centre for educational research and innovation

ADULT ILLITERACY
AND ECONOMIC PERFORMANCE

Ministry of Education, Ontario
Information Services
13th Floor, Mowat Block, Queen's Park
Toronto   M7A 1L2

ORGANISATION FOR ECONOMIC CO-OPERATION AND DEVELOPMENT

ORGANISATION FOR ECONOMIC CO-OPERATION AND DEVELOPMENT

Pursuant to Article 1 of the Convention signed in Paris on 14th December 1960, and which came into force on 30th September 1961, the Organisation for Economic Co-operation and Development (OECD) shall promote policies designed:

— to achieve the highest sustainable economic growth and employment and a rising standard of living in Member countries, while maintaining financial stability, and thus to contribute to the development of the world economy;
— to contribute to sound economic expansion in Member as well as non-member countries in the process of economic development; and
— to contribute to the expansion of world trade on a multilateral, non-discriminatory basis in accordance with international obligations.

The original Member countries of the OECD are Austria, Belgium, Canada, Denmark, France, Germany, Greece, Iceland, Ireland, Italy, Luxembourg, the Netherlands, Norway, Portugal, Spain, Sweden, Switzerland, Turkey, the United Kingdom and the United States. The following countries became Members subsequently through accession at the dates indicated hereafter: Japan (28th April 1964), Finland (28th January 1969), Australia (7th June 1971) and New Zealand (29th May 1973). The Commission of the European Communities takes part in the work of the OECD (Article 13 of the OECD Convention). Yugoslavia, a country with special status in the OECD, takes part in some of its work (agreement of 28th October 1961).

The Centre for Educational Research and Innovation was created in June 1968 by the Council of the Organisation for Economic Co-operation and Development.
The main objectives of the Centre are as follows:

— *to promote and support the development of research activities in education and undertake such research activities where appropriate;*
— *to promote and support pilot experiments with a view to introducing and testing innovations in the educational system;*
— *to promote the development of co-operation between Member countries in the field of educational research and innovation.*

The Centre functions within the Organisation for Economic Co-operation and Development in accordance with the decisions of the Council of the Organisation, under the authority of the Secretary-General. It is supervised by a Governing Board composed of one national expert in its field of competence from each of the countries participating in its programme of work.

Publié en français sous le titre :

L'ILLETTRISME DES ADULTES
ET LES RÉSULTATS ÉCONOMIQUES

© OECD 1992
Applications for permission to reproduce or translate all or part of this publication should be made to:
Head of Publications Service, OECD
2, rue André-Pascal, 75775 PARIS CEDEX 16, France

FOREWORD

This volume forms a part of the on-going work in the CERI project "Technological Changes and Human Resources Development". Previous work under the project has demonstrated clearly the new skills that are needed in the workforce in order to realise the full potential of new technologies. The present work focuses on literacy. It considers the evidence that a large proportion of workers have literacy skills below what is required in their daily lives, examines the implications for the economy and asks how best adult literacy can be upgraded.

The study was carried out by Ms Lauren Benton and Mr. Thierry Noyelle of the Eisenhower Center for the Conservation of Human Resources at Columbia University, New York. It was guided by an international group of experts co-ordinated by the CERI Secretariat, which met three times during the course of the work. The authors are indebted to the members of this group, who provided background materials instrumental in the preparation of the manuscript, and extremely useful comments and criticisms on early drafts. The report is published on the responsibility of the OECD Secretary-General.

ALSO AVAILABLE

Education and the Economy in a Changing Society (1989)
(91 88 03 1) ISBN 92-64-13176-0 FF80 £10.00 US$17.00 DM33

Human Resources and Corporate Strategy. Technological Change in Banks and Insurance Companies: France, Germany, Japan, Sweden, United States *by Olivier Bertrand, Thierry Noyelle* (1988)
(96 88 01 1) ISBN 92-64-13096-9 FF70 £8.50 US$15.50 DM31

Information Technologies and Basic Learning. Reading, Writing, Science and Mathematics (1987)
(96 87 05 1) ISBN 92-64-13025-X FF150 £15.00 US$32.00 DM65

Labour Market Policies for the 1990s (1990)
(81 90 01 1) ISBN 92-64-13363-1 FF110 £13.00 US$23.00 DM43

Cut along dotted line

ORDER FORM

Please enter my order for:

Qty.	Title	OECD Code	Price
......	....	....	....
......	....	....	....
......	....	....	....
......	....	....	....

Total : ....

- Payment is enclosed ☐
- Charge my VISA card ☐ Number of card ....
  (Note: You will be charged the French franc price.)
  Expiration of card .... *Signature* ....
- Send invoice. A purchase order is attached ☐

Send publications to *(please print)*:
   Name ....
   Address ....
   ....
   ....

Send this Order Form to OECD Publications Service, 2, rue André-Pascal, 75775 PARIS CEDEX 16, France, or to OECD Publications and Information Centre or Distributor in your country *(see last page of the book for addresses)*.

Prices charged at the OECD Bookshop.

THE OECD CATALOGUE OF PUBLICATIONS and supplements will be sent free of charge
on request addressed either to OECD Publications Service,
or to the OECD Distributor in your country.

CONTENTS

Preface 7

Chapter 1. INTRODUCTION 9

Chapter 2. LITERACY AND ECONOMIC PERFORMANCE IN CONTEXT 13

    Skills and economic performance in the new global economy 13
    Literacy and the workforce 14
    The rise of the concept of functional literacy 16
    Functional literacy 18
    Notes and references 21

Chapter 3. THE SCOPE OF THE LITERACY PROBLEM IN INDUSTRIALIZED NATIONS 23

    The development of direct literacy assessment surveys in the United States 23
    Canada: The first nation-wide Literacy Assessment Survey 24
    Publicity produces a literacy assessment in France 27
    Action precedes assessment in the United Kingdom 28
    Notes and references 29

Chapter 4. REMEDIAL INTERVENTIONS BY PUBLIC SECTOR AND VOLUNTARY INSTITUTIONS 31

    The lack of federal leadership and the limits of decentralization: The politics of literacy in the United States 32
    Decentralization and local experimentation: The federal and provincial roles in Canada ... 35
    Reconciling national guidelines with local autonomy: Adult education and adult literacy in Sweden 37
    Searching for an appropriate delivery model: The fight for literacy in France 39
    The United Kingdom's "bottom-up" literacy movement 40
    Awaiting national awareness: The Federal Republic of Germany 40
    Overview 41
    Notes and References 43

Chapter 5. LITERACY, PRODUCTIVITY, AND GROWTH. CONTEXTUAL REMEDIAL LITERACY TRAINING 45

    The economic cost of illiteracy 46
    Union participation 47
    Curriculum reform 50
    Restructuring work as a training strategy 51
    Learner-centered strategies 52
    Overview 53
    Notes and references 54

Chapter 6. CONCLUSION 57

Annex 1: CANADA'S SURVEY OF LITERACY SKILLS USED IN DAILY ACTIVITIES: SURVEY PREPARATION AND MEASUREMENT ISSUES
by Alvin Satin, Karen Kelly, Gilles Montigny and Stan Jones 59

Background 59
Survey objectives and data requirements of Canada's Survey of Literacy Skills Used in Daily Activities (LSUDA) 59
Conceptualizing literacy 60
Data collection instruments and methods 61
The functional literacy continuum 63
Measuring functional literacy 64
Conclusion 66
Notes and references 67

Annex 2: DIRECT VERSUS PROXY MEASURES OF ADULT FUNCTIONAL LITERACY: A PRELIMINARY RE-EXAMINATION
by David Neice and Margaret Adsett, with Wesley Rodney 69

Purpose 69
Concepts 70
The use of proxy measures 70
Direct assessment and the Statistics Canada Survey of Literacy Skills 72
LSUDA reading skill levels and educational attainment 76
LSUDA reading skill levels and self-assessment of literacy skills 78
LSUDA reading skill levels and frequency of reading 80
LSUDA reading skill levels and self-assessment of adequacy of workplace literacy skills 82
LSUDA reading skill levels and other proxy indicators 83
Conclusion 84
Notes and references 86

PREFACE

This is the first OECD study on adult illiteracy. It appears at a time when advanced industrialised countries are starting to worry seriously about illiteracy, having previously considered it largely a problem for developing nations. The underlying reason for this new concern is suggested precisely by CERI's work on technological change: it is not that schools are turning out demonstrably less literate graduates than in the past, but that the ways in which adults need to apply literacy skills are becoming far more demanding. But the phenomenon of illiteracy in industrialised countries is as yet relatively little studied or understood; the study that follows is a significant attempt to pull together what is known at the international level.

Specifically, CERI hopes that the study will have an impact at a number of levels. First, it aims to stimulate the growing interest in an important problem. This interest has been raised by International Literacy Year 1990, and is now high on the political agenda of some OECD countries, notably the United States, Canada and France. More countries need to consider the reasons for the concern, while those countries that already worry about illiteracy need to sustain their interest: long-term solutions are needed, possibly including new approaches to the way both children and adults learn. Second, the study aims to stimulate further research. It points out the serious gaps in our knowledge, in particular about the extent of illiteracy and about which of the many types of remedial programme actually succeed in improving adults' literacy skills. Third, by considering what is known in a number of countries, the study could potentially help to spread understanding across borders. Specifically, there may be scope for borrowing internationally some methods of measuring adult literacy, and the two annexes on Canada's work in this area are intended to be of practical use.

Finally, despite the gaps in knowledge, the study aims to contribute substantially to international understanding of literacy and illiteracy. In CERI's view, the single most important lesson of this volume is that literacy is not a problem affecting small, marginal sections of the population, but a central issue determining the competence of the workforce. Estimates vary widely according to definitions, but it is conceivable that about one-third of workers could do their jobs better if they were able to use basic reading and writing skills better. This perspective will inform CERI's continuing work on human resources, which is now focusing on the development of adults as lifelong learners.

Chapter 1
INTRODUCTION

With the growing recognition that literacy levels in the years ahead will intrinsically be tied to the capacity of firms and nations to respond to economic challenges, the opportunity exists in advanced countries for the formation of a broad coalition to support the expansion of literacy training. This is welcome news in a field that has long been characterized by insufficient funding and policy attention as well as fragmentation – both in the implementation of remedial programs and among various schools of researchers and practitioners. Many employers who formerly regarded illiteracy as a minor worry have now begun to view the issue as critically linked to competitiveness. Many educators who once resented any emphasis on the economic impact of literacy training have come to recognize that the best pedagogical methods often include, or even focus on, the working lives and economic goals of learners.

Yet we should not regard as inevitable a strong push for greater attention or resources devoted to enhancing literacy levels in the developed world. Despite signs of strong support for fighting illiteracy, we also find persisting barriers to effective alliance-building among participants in the field. So far, employers often still fail to match rhetoric with significant investments. Many educators continue to resist recasting their programs to make them more effective, particularly if doing so might mean compromising institutional interests. Governments still devote insufficient resources, and often prefer bureaucratic reshuffling to substantive changes in policy. In most cases, learners, too, remain marginalized from decision-making about curriculum and program goals and often fail to grasp their right to have a say in guiding policy. In short, the opportunity may exist for wider consensus and more co-ordinated action, but whether particular local, regional, or national communities will be able to seize this opportunity remains to be seen.

Scope of the book

This monograph presents a composite view of the literacy problem, the linkage between literacy and economic performance, and the opportunities and difficulties for addressing successfully the challenges raised by deficient levels of literacy in a cross-section of OECD countries. The focus is on literacy problems among adults, particularly among those already in the workforce.

The following chapter on "Literacy and Economic Performance in Context" discusses recent changes in the nature of economic competition and the implications of such changes for work, skills, and the linkage between enhanced literacy and improved economic performance. The point is made that most of the industrialized nations of the OECD have entered a new economic era characterized by new industries, new forms of production and competition, and a much higher premium on skills. Those with low levels of literacy and basic workplace skills find it increasingly difficult to obtain or retain employment. And, as we show, the problem of poor literacy and low basic skills is not one that is mostly confined to young, high school dropouts or selected groups of unemployed workers – as is often alleged – but one that is equally serious among older, employed workers.

Still, defining and measuring literacy and basic skill problems in the context of the new economy, for the purpose of remedial intervention, is not a simple matter. In Chapter 2, we also retrace how conceptions and measurements of literacy have evolved over time to arrive at a modern concept of "functional literacy" that seeks to link the literacy performance capabilities of individuals more closely and directly to their everyday needs in civic life and in the workplace.

Chapter 3, "The Scope of the Literacy Problem in Industrialized Nations", takes note of findings from recent and current efforts at direct functional literacy measurement in several OECD Member countries. While only a few countries are currently carrying out such direct assessments, findings from their surveys of literacy levels are extremely useful in clarifying the nature and magnitude of the literacy problem. An important finding from these surveys is that, contrary to popular perceptions, the incidence of illiteracy, when classically defined as the inability to decipher printed words, is actually quite low in industrialized nations. The problem, instead, appears to lie in the alarmingly high incidence of what many observers call "functional illiteracy". High proportions of individuals fall within the lower and middle ranges of literacy scales and, despite some literacy skills, are unable to participate fully in the economic and civic life of today's advanced nations. We discuss these findings and also show how they are being used in some countries by government, employer groups, community organizations, and others concerned with literacy to elevate national consciousness and promote remedial action.

In Chapter 4, "Remedial Interventions by Public Sector and Voluntary Institutions", we examine the institutional arrangements utilized by voluntary and government agencies to deliver literacy training in several OECD countries. Our survey does not claim to be comprehensive, only indicative of the rather wide mix of institutional responses in place in the countries reviewed for the purpose of this analysis. As we suggest in the course of this review, different approaches appear to have different benefits and disadvantages. However, a key issue in almost every country appears to be finding the appropriate balance between central guidance and decentralized program implementation and program innovation. Still, in the absence of extensive assessments by countries of both the effectiveness of various delivery modes and the performance of individual programs (rates of retention, rates of completion, etc.), definitive conclusions as to what constitutes an optimal delivery model or set of models are difficult to draw.

In Chapter 5, "Literacy, Productivity, and Growth", we return to a discussion of the linkage between enhancing literacy and sustaining growth in industrialized countries opened up in Chapter 2. We profile key examples of firm- and sector-based efforts in a number of OECD countries that focus on raising literacy simultaneously with expanding basic workplace skills and, in effect, on strengthening both literacy and economic performance.

Our emphasis is on combining a broad assessment of what is known and what is being done in the field of literacy with an understanding of where remedial efforts might lead, provided they receive sufficient support. While our assessment is based on a review of experiences in several OECD countries, our objective is not to present an exhaustive picture of what is known or done in particular countries. Rather, we discuss individual country experiences only to point to broad themes, issues, trends, and tendencies relative to the literacy problem and likely to be common to most industrialized countries. The imbalance that may be found in our presentation of the materials – with materials from some countries featuring more frequently or more prominently than those from others – must be seen as a result of the often highly patchy nature of the scholarly and policy evidence about the adult literacy issue in OECD countries and not the result of some particular bias on the part of the authors. The unevenness in available scholarly and policy materials itself reflects differences in national perceptions about the seriousness of the problem and varying responses in funding research and assessment efforts.

This is consistent with the conclusion that emerges from the different chapters and is restated in the concluding chapter, namely that the field of adult literacy and economic performance is an area that remains in sore need of measurement and assessment. Indeed, one objective in carrying out this study is to point to fields in which international organizations, such as the OECD, might make significant contributions by promoting cross-national efforts in the areas of public-sector, voluntary, or private-sector intervention, assessment of program and institutional effectiveness, and measurement of the scope of literacy or of the cost of low levels of literacy to economic growth and productivity.

In this respect, one area that is receiving growing attention from educational policy-makers and analysts in a number of OECD countries is the direct measurement of literacy levels in the labor force of industrialized economies. While efforts carried out in the United States, Canada, and France (so far the only countries with direct assessments) are discussed at some length in Chapter 2, we thought it would be helpful if policy-makers and analysts at Statistics Canada and Canada's Department of the Secretary of State with the most recent experience with large-scale measurement of literacy were asked to share with us some of what they have learned (note that Canada has just completed a full-scale literacy assessment of its adult population). Annexes 1 and 2, prepared respectively by Statistics Canada and Canada's Department of the Secretary of State, address the issue of measurement of literacy levels in advanced economies. Annex 1 focuses on the survey method used by Statistics Canada in its 1989 survey of literacy levels in Canada's adult population. That method is an expansion and refinement of a survey methodology first developed by the Educational Testing Service (ETS) on behalf of the U.S. Department of Education for its 1985 National Assessment of Educational Progress (NAEP) – a study of literacy levels among young U.S. adults (aged 21 to 25). Annex 2 focuses on the development of robust proxy measures that might be used as second-best alternatives to direct survey measurement of literacy levels.

Throughout our work on this project, we have been impressed by the degree to which diverse interests appear to be converging in support of expanding literacy research and training, and encouraging experimentation with new approaches where older methods have failed. However, we have also found that few sources provide policy-makers and practitioners with an overview of the problem and a framework for analyzing widely different and scattered programs. International comparisons are especially lacking. It is our hope that this book begins to respond to this need and can help guide both research and policy in the right directions.

Chapter 2

LITERACY AND ECONOMIC PERFORMANCE IN CONTEXT

Literacy is a social construct whose definition has evolved historically, often in response to broad economic transformations. At the beginning of this century, when a large proportion of jobs required little or no reading and writing, many of the advanced industrial nations would have defined literacy simply as the ability to sign one's name. In both poorer and wealthier nations today, in contrast, the idea of literacy denotes mastery of a much more complex set of tasks. In part, this difference reflects changes in the structure of the economy and in the nature of work; in part, it responds to a more subtle understanding of literacy requirements in all social spheres.

Not surprisingly, reasons for promoting literacy have changed over time (and have varied across countries). In much of northern Europe and the United Kingdom, for example, literacy – and the right of individuals to achieve literacy – was for a long time linked closely with the goal of full participation (and, specifically, voting) by the people in "civic" life. More recently, particularly in the United States, the emphasis has shifted strongly in favor of a view of literacy as essential to economic performance, both of individuals and of local and national economies. This recent trend responds to important shifts in the nature of the world economy and related changes in the organization and sectoral distribution of jobs.

Skills and economic performance in the new global economy

Most observers of the economy would agree that the middle of the 1970s marked a shift from the post-war Fordist era, characterized by the domination of mass production and the vertically integrated firm to an era of more intense global competition involving more complex and more flexible production networks. This shift has had important implications for the organization of work. Within firms, the Fordist approach centered on the pursuit of a highly fragmented division of labor and the breakdown of work into sets of simple, easy to learn tasks so that workers could be made interchangeable or, for that matter, could be replaced by machinery. Facing more competitive, more fragmented, and highly volatile markets, many firms in the late 1970s and especially the 1980s responded by altering the structure of production in order to emphasize quality, diversification, customization, timeliness, rapid innovation, and customer service[1]. Although sustaining high levels of productivity remains critical, the *quality* of work exacted from employees has become at least as important as the *quantity*. Not surprisingly, it is now widely recognized that firms face intense pressures to enhance the skill level of the workforce[2]. Strategies to achieve this goal include more selective recruitment and accelerated technological change to displace poorly skilled workers; they also emphasize increasingly improvements through training and retraining of the existing workforce.

The new emphasis on skills as a major factor of competitiveness has played a key role in propelling the issue of literacy to the fore of the policy debate. Although considerable attention has been devoted to the problem of defining literacy in general (mainly with the aim of altering our notion of literacy to respond to the new economic context), efforts have turned increasingly towards enriching our understanding of the problem by providing empirical studies in which to ground these more philosophical debates. For example, key questions such as how the problem of illiteracy relates to social stratification, on the one hand, and job characteristics, on the other (to say nothing of workers' welfare), play a larger role today in guiding research and in structuring policy debates. Nevertheless, as this monograph will show, much remains to be done, particularly if we are to answer another set of questions relating to program design and effectiveness, and the overall costs of illiteracy in terms of lost production and lost competitiveness.

This monograph reports on how far we have come in answering key questions regarding illiteracy in OECD countries. Our concern with the implications of the literacy problem for economic performance and, in turn, with the impact of recent economic shifts on both the reality and the conceptualization of the literacy problem, will be apparent to the reader. However, we also hope to contribute to the wider task of assessing the scope of the problem, identifying useful ways of studying it, and calling attention to some promising directions in policy. In this chapter, we address several key points, namely the definition of illiteracy, its distribution in the population, and the impact of economic restructuring on ideas about workforce literacy and performance.

Literacy and the workforce

In today's advanced economies there is an assumption widely shared by policy-makers and the public at large that illiteracy is a phenomenon found mostly among selected groups of unemployed and, more importantly, among marginalized youth who have dropped out of the secondary education system or graduated from it with extremely limited skills.

With the benefit of new insights gained from a recent in-depth survey of the literacy skills of the Canadian population aged 16 to 69, we now know that this view offers only a very partial assessment of the literacy problem in advanced economies. Indeed, a key finding of the Canadian survey (discussed in greater detail in Chapter 3 as well as in Annexes 1 and 2) is that poor literacy is also found in a significant share of the older employed adult workforce.

The Canadian survey breaks down the Canadian population into four groups based on reading levels, with level 1 representing the lowest skill level ("basic illiteracy"), level 4 the highest ("functional literacy"), and levels 2 and 3 intermediate levels of less-than-full functional literacy. What the survey shows is that literacy declines as individuals get older. For example, only 6 per cent of those between the ages of 16 and 24 have reading levels 1 and 2, and only 7 per cent of those 25 to 34 years old, but this proportion rises to 14 per cent for those between ages 35 and 54, and 36 per cent in the oldest, 55 to 64 years old group[3]. In other words, the evidence from the Canadian survey supports a view already shared by educators and cognitive scientists, namely that literacy tends to deteriorate over time, partly because of the individual's insufficient direct use of his or her literacy skills.

This finding is extremely important, not only for Canada but for other advanced economies as well, if we take note of two additional observations: first, that with the ongoing shift to the new global economy, training needs are increasing sharply, not only among entry-level workers, but increasingly also among those already in the workforce who must learn new jobs and/or new ways of doing their old jobs; second, that the notion that the skill level of a nation's workforce can simply be raised through the replacement of its older, less-educated workforce by a younger, better-trained one flies in the face of declining birth rates and of the fact that industrialized nations cannot wait for the coming of age of a new generation of workers to fix the skill problem. Competition demands that countries act faster.

Here again, findings from Canada are helpful in illustrating some of these points. Preliminary findings from a recent two-year longitudinal study carried out in Canada suggest that more than half of the population aged 16 to 64 (55.4 per cent) changed labor force status during the two-year survey period (1986-1987). Conversely, only 44.6 per cent of the labor force either remained in the same jobs or remained unemployed. More precisely, the roughly 8 million Canadians who changed job status made a total of nearly 26 million changes (including changes from employed to unemployed, changes from unemployed to employed, changes of employer, or changes of job within the same enterprise), an average of 3.3 changes per individual over a two-year period. A large number of these job changes was not simply back and forth transitions from employment to unemployment but, instead, job changes among the employed. And, while the incidence of job changes tended to be higher among younger than older workers, nearly one out of every five workers between the ages of 35 and 54 changed job status more than twice during the two-year period. In short, as the Canadian data suggest, labor market flux and the resulting needs in new learning and job training are not limited to younger workers but importantly also include older workers[3].

As for the role of youth in the rejuvenation of the labor force of advanced economies, Statistics Canada recently collected data on the number and percentage of "student entrants" into the labor force of eleven OECD Member countries which shed light on this dimension of the problem. The term "student entrant" picks up not only youth who graduated from school the year before entering the labor market, but also "re-entrants", i.e. individuals who may have returned to school after a period of work and are now ready to re-enter the job market. Still, roughly 90 per cent of those "student entrants" in the eleven countries were under 25.

Statistics Canada's findings are for 1988 and are shown in Table 2.1. On average, student entrants represented only 3.3 per cent of the total labor force of the eleven countries. Only the Netherlands (8.9 per cent of total labor force) deviated significantly from the average. At this average rate of entry, it should take roughly 30 years for mature OECD countries to replace their existing labor force with a better-schooled labor force – hardly the rate of change demanded by today's highly competitive world economy.

To summarize, illiteracy in advanced nations is not a problem that is restricted to a group of mostly drop-out youths, but one that includes also a significant number of older workers. The implications of this finding are fundamental. Remedying to the literacy problem cannot be seen simply in terms of restructuring secondary education so as to cut down in the rate of high school drop-outs, but must also be seen in terms of restructuring remedial programs that are targeted to an older, adult population, including a sizeable share of the *employed* adult labor force. To do so, however, assumes a better understanding of what illiteracy is and what the extent of the problem is. In the remainder of this chapter and in the next one we examine these issues, by looking first at the emergence of the concept of functional literacy and, second, at the development of assessment techniques to measure the extent of functional literacy.

Table 2.1. **Number and share of student entrants into the labor force of selected OECD countries, 1988**

	Number (in thousands)		Student entrants as a share of labor force (%)
	Labor force	Student entrants	
Belgium	3 875	73	1.9
France	23 943	639	2.7
Denmark	2 869	127	4.4
Germany	28 820	485	1.7
Greece	3 961	80	2.0
Ireland	1 322	51	3.9
Luxembourg	155	4	2.5
Netherlands	6 524	582	8.9
Portugal	4 742	90	1.9
Spain	14 608	387	2.6
United Kingdom	28 199	1 153	4.1
Average	–	–	3.3

Source: Information supplied to Statistics Canada by Member countries. From David P. Ross, "Functional Literacy and Labour Markets" (1990).

The rise of the concept of functional literacy

Grade attainment

For some years now, when seeking to define and measure literacy, advanced nations have used educational levels completed by the adult population as the basic measure. The advantage of this method is that data are available in almost all countries, allowing both some comparison among countries and the tracking of historical progress in particular countries. Detailed data on grade attainment exist for most advanced countries, and comparative studies have been prepared by the OECD for its Member countries and Eurostat for EEC member countries. A recent interim report by Eurostat shows grade-level attainment for 14 to 64 year-olds in European countries and gives useful information on relative access to formal education by providing a breakdown of male and female grade completion (see Table 2.2). When these data are analyzed by age group and employment status, they can help in identifying the source of illiteracy problems in the adult population.

These data are limited, however. To begin with, grade school systems are too idiosyncratic to compare easily the content of grade levels from one country to another. In addition, grade completion levels, even if accurately reported by survey respondents, give little indication as to the actual capabilities of the adult population. Some recent findings from Canada help illustrate the problem. Researchers using Canadian Census data had come to use ninth-grade completion as a minimum indicator of literacy. However, Statistics Canada's recent survey of literacy as measured through competency tests found that roughly one in eight adults with more years of schooling could be classified as "false literates"; that is, they had completed nine years of schooling but performed at the level of "functional illiterates"[4].

Table 2.2. **Education levels completed by EEC member countries (as a percentage of total labor force), 1988**

Highest education completed	Germany	France	Italy	Belgium	Luxembourg	United Kingdom	Ireland	Denmark	Greece	Portugal	Spain
No formal education	7.18	28.62	1.10		1.17	0.34	1.06		6.51	33.40	21.64
First level		22.95	9.14	38.22	55.19	4.65	39.94	1.84	51.83	49.36	39.69
Second level, first stage	39.40	30.36	68.47	28.91	26.74	65.80	25.36	46.33	8.29	8.89	19.96
Second level, second stage	41.39	6.84	17.47	19.92	8.07	16.17	23.21	38.31	20.13	4.39	12.02
Third level			3.82		2.59						6.69
Third level, non-university	4.76	4.95		9.07	2.18	5.56	5.34	6.23	4.42	1.61	
Third level, university or equivalent	5.94	2.50		3.88	3.66	6.32	4.44	4.46	8.42	2.31	
Post-graduate	1.33	3.79			0.40	1.15	0.66	2.84	0.40	0.05	
Total labor force	100.00	100.00	100.00	100.00	100.00	100.00	100.00	100.00	100.00	100.00	100.00

Source: Eurostat, 1988 Community Labour Force Survey, March 1990.

Reading tests

An improvement on this first measurement approach is to administer standardized tests that measure respondents' grade-level reading abilities. This form of assessment is common to many educational and training programs. In the United States, for example, the Job Partnership Training Act (JTPA) Program routinely uses grade reading levels as measured through tests administered in school as eligibility requirements. And yet, although more meaningful than grade completion data, results from these tests also have serious limitations, especially as predictors of job performance. For example, research conducted for the U.S. military found a low correlation between reading scores and on-the-job performance. Indeed, those who tested poorly performed virtually the same as higher-testing groups in all performance categories during military service, although they tended to be promoted less frequently[5].

The inability to match up tested grade reading levels and job performance has to do both with the kind of testing that has traditionally been used and with the nature of learning itself. Researchers have found that when respondents are familiar with the content of messages, they can read at levels that are two to four grades higher than when they are reading unfamiliar materials. A single individual reading different types of material can also show substantial differences in scoring[6]. Such findings place a greater burden on testers to find ways of evaluating learners that more fairly reflect cultural and linguistic differences and that also relate more closely to the actual contexts in which readers work and live.

Such findings also support a broader understanding of the complex set of behaviors collapsed under the rubric of "literacy". Only at the very lowest reading levels can literacy be described simply as the ability to decode written words or phrases. Even at relatively low levels of requirements, individuals must draw on a wide range of abilities in reading so that they can not only *decipher* messages but also *interpret* them[7]. Literacy appears intricately connected to a series of "second order competencies" that enable individuals to tackle new tasks (applying existing competencies in a new way) or to relate specific tasks to a larger set of goals (combining competencies to solve complex problems).

Functional literacy

It is the recognition of such complexity that has supported revision of the very definition of literacy. The concepts "functional literacy" and "functional illiteracy" were introduced to distinguish the higher-order level of abilities that separates those who are barely able to read and write ("basic illiterates") from those who are able to use their skills to function fully in the workplace, the community, and at home ("functional literates"). UNESCO's definition of literacy attempted to capture this meaning:

"A person is functionally literate who can engage in all those activities in which literacy is required for effective functioning of his/her group and community and also for enabling him/her to continue to use reading, writing and calculation for his/her own and the community's development."[8]

Increasingly, government agencies are adhering to this meaning, even when they must also adopt narrower operational definitions. The influential 1985 National Assessment of Educational Progress (NAEP) study of literacy among young adults in the United States defined literacy as follows:

> "using printed and written information to function in society, to achieve one's goals, and to develop one's knowledge and potential."[9]

Canada's definition used in its 1989 survey of literacy skills is as follows:

> "Information processing skills necessary to use printed materials commonly encountered at work, at home, and in the community"[10].

Such definitions, of course, raise new problems and questions. Some authors have rejected the use of the term "functional illiteracy" because it implies a tighter fit than actually appears to exist between literacy skills and functional competence. Others complain that the term "illiteracy" is often used to describe a condition pertaining to the developing countries, and "functional illiteracy" as pertaining to developed countries, as if the two conditions were different. Still others have observed that the term "functional illiteracy" suggests a high value placed on conformity to specific functional contexts. Each context crystallizes a set of social, political, and power relationships, and simply exhorting participants to function better entails encouraging conformity to its structure. It is no accident, some point out, that the term "functional illiteracy" – and much of the early research supporting its interpretation – originated in the military, where becoming truly "functionally literate" means essentially being a good soldier. In the realm of national or local politics, in contrast, fully functional citizens have analytical and critical abilities that allow them to question the very framework and language in which political issues are presented and discussed[11].

Both the recognition of the importance of the functional context of learning and the idea that conformity to functional contexts is an insufficient goal for public policy have crucial implications for the way we view the link between literacy and economic performance. Understanding literacy as a context-specific competency implies the need for a close linkage between literacy training for adults and workplace and job training. Traditional workplace programs try to help learners by removing them from the job context, giving them general literacy instruction for a few hours per week, and returning them to the workplace. Not only is training thus removed from its functional context but workers are encouraged to conform to job structures, whether or not these make sense; as we shall explain below, worker participation in ordering the production process would represent a much more forward-looking goal, given current competitive conditions.

The challenge of tying literacy training to job training has become even more immediate because of accelerating change in the nature of jobs themselves. Researchers point out that literacy needs in most jobs are already quite high; several studies show that difficulty levels of on-the-job reading materials typically range from ninth to twelfth grade levels, and that only a tiny percentage of jobs require no reading at all[12]. Those workers called upon to do the most reading are workers learning new jobs who may include many with the least amount of previous job-related training[13]. More broadly, analyses of labor market shifts suggest a growing tension between steady growth in advanced economies in jobs requiring reading and communications skills, and the tendency for larger proportions of the labor force to be drawn from groups that have on average completed fewer years of schooling, such as women, minorities, immigrants, or other disadvantaged groups.

The implications of recent trends are still more far-reaching, however. Observers of broad economic shifts in advanced economies note that the accelerating fragmentation and diversification of markets, coupled with intensifying international competition since the mid-1970s, have altered competitive strategies of firms and affected the structure of most jobs.

In manufacturing, the emphasis on training workers to perform routinized tasks in mass production factories has been replaced by a concern for maximizing flexibility and improving communications among production centers. Thus we see not only a need by some firms to recruit more highly educated workers but also a desire to recast traditional roles in the factory in such a way that existing workers are called upon to perform a range of new, literacy-requiring tasks.

In the services, the fastest growing sector of the developed economies, the demand for new types of workers is also striking. Although there has been inordinate attention to the rapid creation of jobs for low-level service workers, this trend represents only a small part of the story. In a process that has paralleled restructuring in manufacturing, the services have also been reorganized internally in response to pressures to diversify products and meet new international competition. One result has been a flattening of organizational structure so that a larger percentage of the service workforce must engage directly in sales and customer service and must, as a consequence, master a higher level of communications skills; another effect has been to enhance the importance of firm-specific technologies and procedures as a way for firms to identify themselves in the market place, with the result that workers are increasingly called upon to master not just generic basic skills but also an array of specific competencies that allow them to understand, apply, and represent firm practices successfully[14].

The growing emphasis on context-related instruction, then, is coming at a time when the context of most jobs is rapidly changing. The locus and nature of change place a higher value on "second-order competencies" and at the same time demand higher minimum basic skills. That is, not only must workers have better skills merely to "function" in the workplace, but they are in fact being called upon to contribute more to firm performance by being able to understand their place in the production process and improvise improvements. The degree to which workers have been able to spur innovation "from below" has varied substantially across regions and sectors within OECD countries; however, where examples of dynamic growth through multi-level innovation have occurred, they have generally been supported by work environments that encourage worker mobility, open-ended educational opportunities, and active learning on the job[15].

In sum, one implication of recent findings about both the nature of literacy and the changing structure of work is that more may have to be done to restructure jobs in ways that will reinforce broad-based learning, just as educational programs must pay closer attention to adult workers' experiences on the job. We will have more to say about this convergence, and about some attempts to bring it about, in a later chapter. In this chapter, we have attempted to emphasize the important changes that have swept the world of work in recent years, and their possible implications for opening communication among economic analysts, cognitive scientists, and education researchers, on the one hand, and greater collaboration among firms, learners, educators, and governments concerned with both literacy and economic growth, on the other. By recognizing the importance of both historical and social contexts in determining the meaning and uses of literacy, we have sought to open the possibility of addressing the literacy problem in ways that recognize local differences, cultural diversity, and participant needs, while responding to economic priorities.

NOTES AND REFERENCES

1. Anthony P. Carnevale, "Put Quality to Work: Train America's Workforce" (Washington, D.C.: American Society for Training and Development, 1990).

2. The upskilling associated with the shift to the new, post-industrial economy was anticipated in the mid-1980s by Michael Piore and Charles Sabel in *The Second Industrial Divide* (New York: Basic Books, 1984), and by other researchers based in a number of OECD countries. The implications for initial skill levels and firm-based training of the workforce have, by now, been researched and discussed by a number of researchers, including the authors of this monograph. See, for example, Olivier Bertrand and Thierry Noyelle, *Human Resources and Corporate Strategy* (Paris: OECD, 1988), reporting on upskilling in the financial sector in the context of work carried out for the OECD; and Lauren Benton, Thomas Bailey, Thierry Noyelle and Thomas M. Stanback Jr., *Employee Training and U.S. Competitiveness: Lessons for the 1990s* (Boulder, CO: Westview Press, 1991), on the implications of upskilling for training in the textile, retail, business service and banking industries.

3. David P. Ross, "Functional Literacy and Labour Markets: Some Findings and Policy Implications", a report to Statistics Canada, August 1990.

4. See Annex 2 for more data on this point.

5. Thomas Sticht, *Reading for Working: A Functional Literacy Anthology* (Alexandria, Virginia: Human Resources Research Organization, 1975).

6. W. Diehl and Larry Mikulecky, "The Nature of Reading at Work", *Journal of Reading* 24 (1980): 221-227; Thomas Sticht, L. Armijo, R. Weitzman, N. Koffman, K. Roberson, F. Chang and J. Moracco, *Teachers, Books, Computers and Peers: Integrated Communications Technologies for Adult Literacy Development* (Monterey, California: U.S. Naval Postgraduate School, 1986).

7. Larry Mikulecky, "Basic Skills Impediments to Communication between Management and Hourly Employees", *Management Communication Quarterly* (May 1990).

8. UNESCO, "Statement of the International Committee of Experts on Literacy" (Paris: UNESCO, 1962).

9. Irwin Kirsch and Ann Jungeblut, *Literacy: Profiles of America's Young Adults*, National Assessment of Educational Progress (Princeton, NJ: Educational Testing Services, 1986).

10. Statistics Canada, Special Survey Groups, *A National Survey on Literacy Skills of Canadian Adults, Background Information*, June 1989.

11. Suzanne de Castell, Allan Luke and David MacLennan, "On Defining Literacy", in *Literacy, Society and Schooling*, eds. Suzanne de Castell, Allan Luke and Kieran Egan (Cambridge: Cambridge University Press, 1986), pp. 3-14.

12. W. Diehl and Larry Mikulecky, 1980, *op. cit.*, T. Rush, A. Moe and R. Storlie, *Occupational Literacy* (Delaware: International Reading Association, 1986); Thomas Sticht, *Basic Skills in Defense* (Virginia: Human Resources Research Organization, 1982).

13. R.P. Kern, "Modeling Users and Their Use of Technical Manuals", in *Designing Usable Texts*, eds. T.M. Duffy and R. Waller (New York: Academic Press, 1985).

14. We will discuss restructuring and its implications for literacy in more detail below. For an analysis of restructuring and worker training in the United States, see Lauren Benton, Thomas Bailey, Thierry Noyelle and Thomas M. Stanback Jr., *Employee Training and U.S. Competitiveness: Lessons for the 1990s, op. cit.*
15. This argument is implicit in much of the literature on flexible production in fast-growing developed economies. See especially Michael Piore and Charles Sabel, *The Second Industrial Divide, op. cit.* For more explicit treatment of this argument in a specific case, see Vittorio Capecchi, ''The Informal Economy and the Development of Flexible Specialization in Emilia Romagna'', in *The Informal Economy,* eds. Alejandro Portes, Manuel Castells and Lauren Benton (Baltimore: Johns Hopkins University Press, 1989).

Chapter 3

THE SCOPE OF THE LITERACY PROBLEM IN INDUSTRIALIZED NATIONS

Measurement of literacy may be presented as a merely technical task, but in reality it is also a highly political one. On the one hand, estimates of illiteracy showing that the magnitude of the problem is pervasive and growing tend to function as a call to action. Thus proponents of strong literacy efforts can often be found citing estimates of the illiterate population that are of questionable accuracy in order to attract attention to the cause. On the other hand, business, government, and community leaders may have incentives to minimize estimates of the problem. Given the increasing attention to the linkages between literacy levels and economic growth, suggestions that illiteracy affects large portions of the workforce may become a threat to a region's ability to attract further investment. More broadly, recognizing the seriousness of the illiteracy problem often implies radically revising national myths about educational standards and about the distribution of wealth and opportunity. These concerns encourage a conservative and critical attitude towards literacy assessments.

There are, of course, very real technical difficulties in conducting accurate assessments of literacy. As noted in the previous chapter, recent research tells us that the most useful representation of the illiteracy problem in the context of advanced nations needs to measure not simply reading and writing skills but also communication, interpretive, and numeracy skills, and, moreover, needs to do so by taking into account the context within which individuals put those skills to use. Data on grade completion of the kind presented in the previous chapter are insufficient for this more complex measurement task. Taking note of the shortcomings of traditional measurement, and responding to research supporting a more contextual approach to literacy, three OECD Member countries have recently sponsored direct assessments of contextual literacy skills: the United States, Canada, and France.

The development of direct literacy assessment surveys in the United States

One approach to assessment that is likely to grow in influence throughout the OECD was initiated in the United States and is now being pursued also by Canada and France, involving direct performance assessment of a broad range of literacy skills through in-depth survey of sample populations. The origins of this work can be linked back to an assessment survey conducted in the United States in the mid-1970s, namely the 1975 Adult Performance Level (APL) survey. Although the 1975 APL survey helped pioneer a methodology using "performance tasks" as indicators of literacy competency, this initial study resulted in the dissemination of figures that proved to be glaringly inaccurate, including one claim that by the year 2000 two out of three Americans would be illiterate. The national estimates based loosely on the APL survey did stimulate interest in the illiteracy problem, however, and, for that reason, received less critical scrutiny than they should have. More importantly, the press and public reliance on APL figures pointed to the need for more reliable estimates based on other large-scale studies[1].

In 1985, the U.S. Department of Education sponsored a special survey of young adults (aged 21 to 25), the National Assessment of Educational Progress (NAEP)[2]. This survey was ground-breaking in its more complex approach to literacy testing. The survey sought to measure three different types of competencies: prose literacy, document literacy, and quantitative literacy. The survey proposed to do so, moreover, without adopting any firm cut-off points for "illiteracy" or "functional illiteracy", but instead by presenting respondents' abilities along three different scales (corresponding to the different types of competency).

The results of the survey suggested two important conclusions. One was that literacy skills were distributed in the population in a way that was consistent with the distribution of economic opportunity. Black young adults performed significantly below white young adults, while Hispanics registered scores that averaged about mid-way between these groups. The second important finding was that the simple inability to read – "illiteracy" as classically defined – appeared far less prevalent than difficulties in using literacy skills to perform simple tasks. Only about 2 per cent of young adults had such limited literacy skills that they were judged to be unable to perform the simplest simulation tasks included in the survey, but, at the same time, only 10 to 40 per cent were able to complete the most complex, multistep tasks; the largest group fell within the middle range of the literacy scales and clearly represented the most troubling category from the perspective of employment policy.

Building on the 1985 NAEP study, the U.S. Department of Labor commissioned the Educational Testing Service (ETS) to develop and conduct literacy assessments of three special populations: unemployment insurance claimants, employment service claimants, and participants in the Job Training Partnership Act. Also underway is preparatory work on a national adult literacy assessment for individuals aged 16 to 64, also to be conducted by ETS for the U.S. Department of Education in 1992. The 1992 assessment will permit for the first time in the United States tracking trends in literacy by comparing the performance of young adults in 1985 with those in 1992. Comparisons will also be made with the 1989 data from the three special surveys sponsored by the Department of Labor. States are being encouraged to participate in this national assessment so that officials can obtain data that will be statistically significant for their states and use the results to inform state policy.

Because they approach literacy measurement in a more complex way, the NAEP survey and other ongoing literacy assessments are gaining considerable influence internationally. A similar approach has been adopted by Canada in two recent assessments (1987 and 1989).

Canada: The first nation-wide Literacy Assessment Survey

Prior to the introduction of these performance task assignments, Canada, like other countries, relied on traditional measures. For example, researchers working with data from the Canadian Census and the Canadian Association for Adult Education (CAAE) both defined functional literacy as equivalent to the completion of nine years of schooling. But a path-breaking survey conducted for *Southam News,* a daily Canadian newspaper, in 1987 provided a first attempt at direct assessment[3]. Interviews were conducted with 2 398 adults; items were adapted from the NAEP English survey instrument and a French version was also prepared.

Instead of reporting the results along the three literacy scales used in the NAEP survey, the *Southam News* study relied on a literacy "jury" to determine what levels of performance should be used as indicators of functional illiteracy[4].

The *Southam News* survey was important in calling attention to the problem of illiteracy in Canada and also in pointing to the need for a more elaborate national assessment. Some of the results were surprising; others, disturbing; and a few were questionable given the shortcomings of the survey methodology. Four and a half million Canadians – or nearly 24 per cent of the Canadians 18 years and older – were judged to be functionally illiterate. The survey also showed that illiteracy decreases from East to West and that there was a higher incidence among children of the jobless, the working class, and the most poorly educated. One controversial finding was that francophones showed higher illiteracy rates than anglophones, a conclusion that was challenged by some critics who complained that the survey instrument had merely been translated from English to French without taking into account respondents' different cultural and functional contexts[5]. Lastly, about half of those labelled as functional illiterates in the survey were found to have completed nine years of schooling and could have been considered literate by more traditional measures.

The *Southam News* survey spurred interest in developing a more sophisticated national assessment for Canada. Subsequently, Statistics Canada conducted a nation-wide survey on behalf of the National Literacy Secretariat in October 1989. The survey assessed a representative sample of about 9 500 individuals between ages 16 to 69. The study was structured to produce a separate test score for each respondent in reading, writing, and numeracy that would allow the individual to be placed in one of four skill-level categories.

As the first such large-scale national assessment of the entire adult population to be completed, the Canadian study will surely be examined closely in other countries where national surveys are under consideration. Findings from the tests on reading and numeracy ability became available in May and July 1990, and complete results appeared later that year. Not surprisingly, the findings confirm general patterns found earlier in the *Southam News* survey, while adding greater detail and precision.

Like the 1987 *Southam News* study (and the 1985 U.S. NAEP survey), reading scores in the 1989 Statistics Canada national assessment suggest that the largest problem is presented by those individuals who can read very simple messages but have severely limited abilities to use their skills to complete complex tasks. Thus when respondents are ranked by level, the following pattern emerges[6]:

Levels	Percent of respondents
Level 1: Canadians at this level have difficulty dealing with printed materials. They most likely identify themselves as people who cannot read [7].	7
Level 2: Canadians at this level can use printed materials only for limited purposes such as finding a familiar word in a simple text. They would likely recognize themselves as having difficulties with common reading materials.	9
Level 3: Canadians at this level can use reading materials in a variety of situations provided the material is simple, clearly laid out and the tasks involved are not too complex. While these people generally do not see themselves as having major difficulties, they tend to avoid situations requiring reading.	22
Level 4: Canadians at this level meet most everyday reading demands. This is a large and diverse group which exhibits a wide range of reading skills.	62

The survey results also reveal a strong correlation between literacy proficiency and educational attainment, age (with younger Canadians outperforming older respondents), and income. Secondary school completion is closely related to the ability to perform everyday reading tasks. Only a small proportion of Canadians who completed secondary education fall in levels 1 and 2 (8 per cent), while over 80 per cent of those who attended universities or community colleges perform at level 4 (see Table 3.1). Differences in educational attainment also appear to explain differences between French- and English-speaking Canadians: while their performance is comparable in the 16 to 24 year old group, older English speakers – who also have a higher secondary school completion rate – performed better on average. Another significant result – and one that confirms the pattern detected in the earlier *Southam News* study – is that reading skills are lowest in the eastern Canadian provinces and highest in the West (see Table 3.2). The lowest reading levels were found in the economically depressed province of Newfoundland, where almost one-quarter of the adult population is at levels 1 and 2, and 36 per cent at level 3; the highest rates are in western provinces such as British Columbia, where only 12 per cent of the adult population falls in levels 1 and 2 while 69 per cent are classified at level 4.

Table 3.1. **Percentage distribution of Canadian adults aged 16-69 by highest level of schooling showing reading skill level**

	Population (thousands)	Level 1	Level 2	Level 3	Level 4
Canada[a]	17 705	5	10	22	63
No schooling or elementary	1 818	27	33	28	12[c]
Some secondary	4 427	3	13	35	48
Secondary completed	4 181	[b]	6[c]	22	70
Trade school	1 133	[b]	[b]	25[c]	63
Community college	2 458	[b]	[b]	15[c]	81
University	3 456	[b]	[b]	8[c]	89

Note: Excludes persons who reported having no skills in either of Canada's official languages. For definition of levels, see text.
 a) Total includes "not stated" level of schooling.
 b) Sampling variability too high for this estimate to be released.
 c) Sampling variability associated with this estimate is high.
Source: "Survey of Literacy Skills Used in Daily Activities", Statistics Canada, 1989.

It is clear, even without going into further detail on the Canadian findings, that this study will provide information of considerable value in determining policy measures to combat illiteracy. A further advantage of this assessment, and of those being conducted or at the planning stage in the United States, is that they will permit some tracking of national trends if or when surveys are repeated.

Given the political usefulness of such assessments, it remains something of a surprise that more efforts are not underway in other OECD countries to produce similar studies. Observers point out that in northern European countries – particularly in Scandinavia and in the former

Table 3.2. **Percentage distribution of persons aged 16-69 by reading skill levels, Canada and provinces**

	Population (thousands)	Level 1	Level 2	Level 3	Level 4
Canada	18 024	7	9	22	62
Atlantic	1 546	6	13	30	52
Newfoundland	384	7	17	36	39
Prince Edward Island	85	a	a	a	a
Nova Scotia	594	5[b]	10	28	57
New Brunswick	483	6	12	26	56
Quebec	4 721	6	13	25	57
Ontario	6 689	9	8	21	62
Prairies	2 984	4	7	19	70
Manitoba	703	5[b]	7[b]	23	65
Saskatchewan	632	3[b]	5[b]	19	72
Alberta	1 649	4	7[b]	17	71
British Columbia	2 084	5	7	19	69

Note: Persons who have reported having no skills in either of Canada's official languages are included in level 1. For definition of levels, see text.
  a) Sampling variability too high for this estimate to be released.
  b) Sampling variability associated with this estimate is high.
Source: "Survey of Literacy Skills Used in Daily Activities", Statistics Canada, 1989.

West Germany – the lack of interest in conducting national assessments is related to the widespread perception that illiteracy is a problem affecting mainly "marginal" populations, particularly immigrants. The push to recognize literacy as a national priority has tended to come largely from volunteer bodies and non-governmental interest groups, not from government[8]. But the reasoning behind the official view is somewhat circular. Short of a full-scale assessment, it is nearly impossible to check whether or not the official view on literacy is indeed accurate.

Publicity produces a literacy assessment in France

This situation may be changing, however. In France, the official position changed rather radically in 1984 with the release of a report to the Prime Minister entitled *Des illettrés en France*[9]. Earlier, France had routinely reported to international agencies, as it did in 1979 to a commission of the European Community, that the country did not have a serious adult illiteracy problem. Also, although France had provisions in place to aid workers in receiving lifelong education, the benefits tended to accrue to non-French speakers. The first official recognition of a problem came in a 1981 report on poverty in France (the Oheix Report)[10], which was followed by the formation of a commission to prepare the 1984 study. The latter report listed numerous recommendations, including establishing an interministerial committee to co-ordinate literacy programs, and an assessment of current levels of provision of services and training.

The publicity surrounding the report's publication established the figure of 2 million adult illiterates in France. This figure, still often cited as the working estimate, was supplemented by findings from a survey in 1986-87 that reported respondents' abilities to speak, read, write and master (understand and use) language. That study concluded that illiteracy affected 1.4 million immigrants and 1.9 million French-born citizens, or a total of 3.3 million adults (over the age of 18) living in France (or 9 per cent of the 37 million persons 18 years and older). Unlike the U.S. and Canadian studies, however, the survey used a small number of indicators of illiteracy, including such items as respondents' reporting on whether they had read a book recently or habitually read the newspaper. Direct assessment of speaking and comprehension relied on interviewers' evaluations[11].

Following these earlier efforts, France has now refined its definition of functional illiteracy. Its current working definition is that of "individuals with difficulties in mastering basic skills" (*personnes en difficulté de maîtrise des savoirs de base*). Five basic skill areas are included under the new working definition:

   i) The capacity to reason (hypothesis formation; anticipation of answers; ability to reason from different points of views; anticipation of cause and consequences);
   ii) The capacity to communicate (reading, writing, verbal);
   iii) Numeracy capacity (counting, measuring, and comparing quantities);
   iv) The capacity to understand time (understand kinship, social group, calendar); and
   v) The capacity to understand space.

France has recently conducted a large-scale assessment of these skills with a sample of 1 500 long-term unemployed 25 years or older from six major cities: Paris, Marseilles, Lyon, Lille, Strasbourg and Toulouse. The survey was conducted between March and May 1990 and the analysis of the results and the publication of findings were projected for summer 1991. This follows an earlier sample survey of a small group of young military draftees using the same survey instrument.

Action precedes assessment in the United Kingdom

Of course, we should not be overly critical of efforts to promote estimates of illiteracy that are not based on direct and complete assessments. As was mentioned earlier, in the United Kingdom, for example, proponents of literacy initiatives began in the 1970s to refer routinely to the figure of 2 million as an estimate of British adults with literacy problems. Public recognition of the problem not only preceded that in France, but large-scale literacy programs also got an earlier start, in part because a promotional campaign led by the BBC drew attention to the issue. There is some indication here too, however, that a national study would have assisted policy-makers. Early promotional efforts and most programs targeted working-class males on the assumption that this group represented the largest number of illiterates. Only recently have programs begun to reach out more aggressively to other groups as policy-makers have realized that the problem is not limited to the original target population.

In summary, then, the goal of producing measurements of illiteracy based on national assessments has been pursued unevenly among OECD Member countries. The United States and Canada have moved farthest towards this goal, while some European countries have only recently begun to address the need for more accurate estimates. Preliminary results from the United States and Canada suggest that assessments can provide information that will be extremely useful in guiding policy, particularly in identifying target populations. By identifying groups and regions most in need, by exploring the range of factors tied to high illiteracy rates, and by characterizing more accurately the nature of literacy difficulties, such studies can help inform decisions about program scope, location, and content. It must be stated, at the same time, that there is no need to postpone action until such assessments can be completed. Literacy campaigns in the United Kingdom, recent government actions in France, and the expansion of the adult education system in Sweden (more on this below) have all responded to a growing recognition of a literacy or basic skills problem in the absence of large-scale, direct assessments.

NOTES AND REFERENCES

1. The APL survey itself should not be blamed for some of the erroneous claims it apparently spawned. The levels of ability needed to perform tasks similar to those used in the survey were generally confirmed in other studies of functional illiteracy in the 1970s: the Survival Literacy study, the Adult Functional Reading Study, the Mini-Assessment of Functional Literacy, and reports from the military in project REALISTIC.
2. Irwin Kirsch and Ann Jungeblut, *Literacy: Profiles of America's Young Adults,* NAEP (Princeton, NJ: Educational Testing Services, 1986).
3. *Southam News,* "Broken Words: A Special Southam Survey" (Toronto, 1987).
4. Critics of the survey's reliance on a jury point out that the cut-off point dividing "literate" and "illiterate" Canadians was necessarily subjective and somewhat arbitrary. See Serge Wagner, "Analphabétisme et alphabétisation au Canada français", Université du Québec à Montréal, November 1987. In fact, the jury in the *Southam News* survey originally suggested a standard of 64 per cent correct answers out of 38 tested items. By this standard, 37 per cent of adult Canadians would have been classified as illiterate, compared with the 24 per cent defined as illiterate in English or French by a more lenient criterion used in the study's final report.
5. Serge Wagner, "Analphabétisme et alphabétisation au Canada français", 1987, *ibid.*
6. For a more detailed description of how these levels were defined and measured, see Stan Jones, "Guide to Literacy Levels on the Survey of Literacy Skills Used in Daily Activities", paper prepared for Statistics Canada, May 1990. See also Annex 1.
7. Persons who reported having no skills in either of Canada's two official languages are reported in level 1.
8. Leslie Limage, "Adult Literacy Policy in Industrialized Countries", in *National Literacy Campaigns,* eds. R. Arnove and H. Graff (Plenum Publishing, United Kingdom, 1987).
9. Véronique Espérandieu and Antoine Lion, *Des illettrés en France* (Paris: La Documentation française, 1984).
10. Gabriel Oheix, "Contre la précarité et la pauvreté: 60 propositions" (Paris: Conseil d'Etat, February 1981).
11. "Etude des conditions de vie des ménages", *INSEE PREMIERE,* No. 27, June 1989.

Chapter 4

REMEDIAL INTERVENTIONS BY PUBLIC SECTOR AND VOLUNTARY INSTITUTIONS

Related to the need for national literacy assessments is the goal of evaluating learners' levels and their progress in remedial literacy programs. Learner assessment and program evaluation are notoriously inconsistent, not to say inadequate, in most cases. Few broad studies exist to guide policy-makers' choices in funding one type of program over another. In part, the difficulty reflects real obstacles in designing assessment and evaluation criteria or instruments; in part, the problem stems from the conflict of interest that arises when institutions or program providers are asked to evaluate their own performance. In particular in countries or regions where volunteers have taken a lead role in the fight against illiteracy, the issue of assessment can be very sensitive.

Some evidence from the United States suggests that many institutions may in fact have much to hide. One recent study of U.S. programs found that many remedial programs have little impact on most learners. While an average of 100 contact hours is needed for a learner to make a one-year gain in grade-level reading ability, no program is reported to hold average learners for that long; overall, only 20 per cent of learners stay for a year or longer[1]. Many programs, in fact, have little incentive to report accurately on completion and success rates. In most states, for example, community college-based literacy programs receive funding according to gross enrolment figures, not according to completion rates or student performance. Taken together, existing programs also appear to reach only a small fraction of the potential pool of learners. By one estimate, only three to four million people in the United States are reached each year, and the average expenditure per learner is under $200, compared with $4 000 per year for each child in public school[2].

For the other developed countries examined here, still less information seems available on the effectiveness and scope of existing programs. Clearly, evaluation is one area of comparative research that is sorely in need of greater attention. Studies of failed programs would be potentially as useful as profiles of programs that work well.

The lack of objective guidelines about what to do to combat illiteracy is just one constraint facing policy-makers. In the countries examined here, policy directions are also heavily influenced by the structure of political authority. This constraint manifests itself in several ways. Actions on literacy can be particularly sensitive to political tensions between regional (or local) and national levels of government. A strong commitment to action on illiteracy at either of these levels is no guarantee that relevant policies will be aggressively implemented if support is withheld elsewhere. In addition, at each level, literacy is an issue which tends not to fall squarely under the purview of a particular agency or leadership. Thus bureaucratic reshuffling as a response to the problem is a common, if not continual, occurrence.

Comparing examples of government response to illiteracy in several countries will help to make these and other points clearer.

The lack of federal leadership and the limits of decentralization: The politics of literacy in the United States

In the United States, responsibility for literacy programs lies mostly at the state level, although partial funding for many programs comes through the federal government and is matched or augmented by state funding. The federal role is, for a number of reasons, not particularly clear-sighted or effective. To begin with, efforts to improve literacy fall under the purview of at least three federal agencies – Education, Labor, and Health and Human Services. Some additional funding is spent by the U.S. Department of Justice as part of its administration of the Immigration Act – mostly on English as a Second Language (ESL) programs[2]. State officials frequently complain that they do not know which agency – and which department within it – to contact with questions about programs or funding for adult literacy. Further, like other funding areas of a non-military nature, adult literacy has not received high funding priority during the last decade. At the federal level, an estimated $1 to $2 billion are spent on a variety of programs, and considerable burden is placed on the states to come up with the bulk of funding[2]. Leadership at the federal level has also not signalled this issue as a high priority, although some recent changes are positive, including the greater attention on literacy from the White House, recent efforts of the U.S. Department of Labor to fund workplace literacy projects, and the recent creation of a five-year Center for Adult Literacy based at the University of Pennsylvania and jointly funded by the U.S. Departments of Education, Labor, and Health and Human Services.

The lack of consistent federal support has complicated matters for the states, some of which have recently made commitments to promote literacy training more actively. For the states, the issue is inextricably tied to economic interests. In a context of declining traditional manufacturing, state officials have become more vocal about the need to raise educational levels in order to support growth strategies focused on promoting services and attracting high-technology investments. What state reformers confront, however, is a highly fragmented funding system that distributes responsibility for adult literacy training among the Job and Training Partnership Act (JTPA), Adult Basic Education (ABE), and a handful of other, smaller programs, some initiated at the state level. In addition to posing administrative difficulties, these divisions often create "turf battles" that can cause agencies to resist reforms designed to improve the overall delivery of services. For example, while experts urge officials to create more programs that blend practical training with basic skills and literacy instruction, vocational education administrators often manoeuver to preserve the relative autonomy, and purity, of more traditional approaches to vocational training.

State officials clearly recognize the need to unify or at least co-ordinate the various state-level programs and funding streams. A brief look at the efforts of three states will give some indication of the range for possible action in this direction and the difficulties states encounter when they try to alter the *status quo*.

In Massachusetts, a change in policy came in 1987, after Governor Dukakis called for increased volunteer efforts to combat illiteracy. At first, the plan was to set up a new office, the Commonwealth Literacy Campaign, to co-ordinate this new volunteer effort. But the very group assigned the initial co-ordinating task became highly critical of traditional approaches relying solely on volunteers. Instead, the group advocated tapping funding from other state agencies to pay professional instructors (and to train volunteers).

The content and style of instruction, however, could not be worked out completely without first solving the difficult problem of who would be eligible for instruction and how access would be arranged. Thus the principal tool of the Coalition became one of co-ordinating actions among state agencies that already dealt with educationally needy populations, such as the social services, welfare, and unemployment offices. A first step was simply to assess the scope of existing literacy programs and to understand which populations were already being served, and which underserved. The Coalition then conducted a statewide survey of existing programs and prepared a comprehensive database. The office planned, later, to try to evaluate which programs were most successful and to use those as models for pilot projects around the state.

However, no sooner had the Coalition's effort been launched in earnest that the plan ran into difficulties. Beginning in 1988, Massachusetts found itself facing a severe budget crisis, and funding for literacy initiatives quickly evaporated. Among other plans affected, a handful of workplace literacy projects had to be curtailed, plans to open regional centers were abandoned, and the Coalition had to limit its role to one of helping to co-ordinate funded literacy programs run by various agencies.

Michigan has fared much better with funding of its new literacy initiative. The plan is part of a broader project started in January 1989 to create a single system of access to all forms of publicly funded basic training. The Michigan Opportunity System will eventually issue cards to all potential recipients and offer them training and education based on their skill levels. Some services will be provided free of charge and others will require partial payment by recipients. The budget for this project includes the state's full budget for adult education, about $230 million, plus another $5 or 6 million in federal funds. The programs involved will be run through a variety of agencies and institutions including JTPA, adult basic education programs, community colleges, and volunteer organizations.

The emphasis of the Michigan project is on workforce literacy. Given the state's declining manufacturing base, state officials perceive a need to prepare the workforce for other, potentially more demanding occupations, as well as for more complex jobs in remaining manufacturing. They understand their role as one of "tearing down turf barriers" to enable disparate agencies to work together. Both state officials and business leaders also want to merge the content of many educational and job training programs, so that basic skills training is more immediately applicable to the workplace. But, as in Massachusetts, the goal of smoothing administrative obstacles seems to be taking precedence over attention to revising the content of literacy instruction. Still, the Michigan effort includes starting a number of pilot projects. These will differ from existing programs mainly in that they will attempt to access all the services available in particular counties and to be more thorough in their identification of target populations. Recipients of welfare, unemployment benefits, and of other state services, will thus be assessed for literacy skills and channelled into literacy programs, most of which will, at least initially, observe traditional techniques. A basic skills training program will also be phased in gradually, as the details of how to assess individuals' skills, place them in appropriate programs, and evaluate their progress are worked out.

Still another strategy for integrating state programs is being tried in Mississippi. Here, too, for quite different reasons, state officials perceive a critical need to bolster economic growth through enhancing citizens' literacy skills. The state is predominantly rural, and has a large poor and undereducated population. Although the state has been somewhat successful in the past in attracting manufacturing firms that were relocating in search of cheaper, non-unionized labor, state officials correctly perceive this strategy to be insufficient for luring high-tech businesses and advanced services to the state. Nor will the availability of low-wage labor be able to attract and hold many traditional manufacturing concerns, whose needs are changing. However, the established system for providing adult education is clearly inadequate to the task of raising educational levels and upgrading skills, particularly because existing programs are run through the state's 15 community colleges, institutions that fail to reach the neediest groups, especially dispersed rural populations with poor access to these sites.

In response to these concerns, Governor Mabus recently established a new Office for Literacy headed by Karl Haigler, a former director of federal adult education in the Reagan administration. The office will serve as an umbrella agency overseeing statewide literacy initiatives. One of its main goals is to establish and follow strict evaluation criteria in refunding existing programs. State officials recognize that the existing system rewards institutions for maintaining enrolment, regardless of how students actually perform and whether or not they complete training. Mississippi has also become the first state to pass a Basic Skills Income Tax Credit that will reward businesses for organizing and funding workplace training programs.

As in Massachusetts and Michigan, state officials also favor changing the relationship between job training and basic skills instruction, with greater overlap in the content of vocational and literacy programs. Yet, as in other states, traditional bureaucratic divisions are perceived to be serious obstacles to this task. The director of the Office for Literacy observes that the "fossilization of thinking" of vocational educators has prevented them from pursuing or supporting innovative approaches that would tie job skills and literacy training. One instructor who designed such an innovative program (a "math for plumbers" course that "even taught trigonometry" by combining mathematics instruction with vocational exercises) was chastised by the state vocational office for altering the traditional curriculum, which contained no basic skills instruction. Such conservative thinking, and the administrative divisions that reinforce it, will change slowly even with aggressive leadership from the Governor's office.

At least in the short run, then, new state initiatives are likely to result in "more of the same" – more literacy programs offered to a wider clientele. Still, the convergence of opinion in these three states about what needs to be done to enhance literacy programs is striking, especially when we consider the significant differences in the three states' economies. In all three, literacy has become an important priority only in the last several years; in all three, interest is tied to economic growth strategies. State officials seem also to agree on the need to co-ordinate better the activities of various state agencies and departments that serve the populations most in need of literacy training. They agree, too, that one substantive change should be to encourage more overlap between vocational and basic skills training. In all three cases, there is a mounting concern, too, with evaluation of programs. The methods for achieving these goals differ considerably, of course, and it would be useful to have further comparative research to weigh the success of various administrative and policy reforms as these efforts mature.

The cases also point to some of the tensions that exist between federal and state-level policy. Our impression is that most state officials view the federal policy as both inefficient and insincere. They find little guidance coming from the federal government about how to achieve integration of separately funded programs, and they have, as a result, begun to look to other states for examples of successful experiments[3]. The cases described here, together with a handful of programs in other states, will probably thus find their importance magnified as other states search for models for action. At the same time, of course, the limitations to state actions remain very real. Budget constraints continually threaten to cut off innovative strategies before they have emerged from infancy, as has already happened to some degree in Massachusetts, and changing political fortunes of influential governors may also adversely affect other experiments. Even where a firm commitment exists and new state agencies have been created, the challenge of sorting out bureaucratic tensions and responsibilities overshadows work on actual program content and design.

Decentralization and local experimentation: The federal and provincial roles in Canada

Provision of training in literacy and basic skills in Canada is even more decentralized than in the United States. There is no officially mandated role for the federal government in primary and secondary education, which is under the direct control of the provinces. The federal government does provide some funding to post-secondary education, and to literacy programs specifically, but support is filtered through several different federal departments. There is no federal Department of Education. The Department of the Secretary of State and the Department of Employment and Immigration show the most active interest in literacy and basic skills. The federal government directly supports Frontier College[4], an institution that, since 1899, has been devoted to enhancing literacy skills of workers and disadvantaged groups (recently, indigenous peoples and the prison population), as well as a number of other programs (including remedial literacy programs for individuals in jail or on parole). In general, however, the federal government is not positioned to play a strong leadership role in the literacy movement, despite growing attention to the links between education and economic performance. The federal role is largely understood to be one of providing services and policy supports that cannot be handled by the provinces; sponsorship of the recent national literacy survey is a prime example[5]. A key principle of the federal effort revolves around the idea of building collaborative efforts through partnerships.

This situation has both advantages and disadvantages. On the positive side, local autonomy allows for experimentation and sometimes adoption of unorthodox or innovative approaches. In comparison with most states in the United States, the Canadian provinces have been on average more supportive of community-based groups and of an overall strategy that favors tailoring programs to community needs. On the negative side, the lack of oversight and strong financial support at the federal level is reflected in a highly uneven, and in some places very undeveloped, infrastructure for delivering training. While a few provinces have been able to provide substantial, consistent funding and have been building literacy programs for over a decade, other provinces have lagged behind and have had to rely on traditional providers – community colleges, local school boards, and volunteer organizations – to take responsibility for adult basic training, whether or not these organizations have proven themselves to be effective providers in the past. A brief comparison of literacy efforts in several provinces illustrates these points.

As was already noted, literacy levels vary substantially by province. The differences reflect in part differences in economic conditions – the poorest provinces are also those with the highest illiteracy rates – and in part variation in other social patterns that influence literacy, such as the proportion of indigenous peoples and immigrants. Provinces with a majority or a sizeable minority of French-speakers also contend with a different historical context for education; among older Canadians, French-speakers tend to have lower illiteracy rates than their English-speaking peers, reflecting the later development of universal secondary education in Catholic institutions. In addition to such variables, the provinces also display bureaucratic-organizational differences that affect both the conception of the literacy issue and the way in which programs are administered.

Not surprisingly, then, we find a wide variety of approaches to the literacy issue. In the Maritime provinces, where illiteracy rates are highest, provincial governments have been the least well prepared to fund sizeable remedial programs. Reliance on volunteer organizations has been much greater here than elsewhere in Canada, in part reflecting the influence of U.S. organizations, principally Laubach of America, and in part because these provinces have relatively few community colleges, traditional providers of most adult education elsewhere in Canada. In contrast, provincial planning to address adult illiteracy has been fairly long-standing in both British Columbia and Quebec, with significantly higher rates of adult literacy.

In British Columbia, planning began in the late 1970s when extensive programming was established through the province's community colleges. For different reasons, Quebec also began organizing a provincial literacy plan in the 1970s. As in other areas of public policy, the province had considerable incentive to establish its autonomy in education policy; not surprisingly, its programs have been characterized by a strong emphasis on distinctive cultural and social contexts as the determinants of both educational achievement and the role that remedial learning should play[6].

Despite these differences in approach, it is fair to say that in virtually all the Canadian provinces, officials are experimenting with an expanding mix of methods to address illiteracy. In British Columbia, for example, officials recognize that the established system of funding literacy training through community colleges is not meeting the needs of many groups; under discussion now is a plan to extend funding to community groups, although the colleges have been successful in retaining control of funding and will oversee community programs. Several provinces have moved much further and faster towards a more "open" system of funding that extends direct support to community groups. Ontario, for example, has established regional centers that oversee funding in their areas and have strong ties to community groups; workplace literacy funds, too, are available from the province not just to the private sector but also to other groups that present successful proposals. Saskatchewan and Manitoba have also begun experimenting with changing administrative structures to allow more direct funding of community groups, particularly since this approach is considered to have more potential for reaching the large indigenous populations in these provinces. The trend towards funding of community-based groups seems to reflect an increasing acceptance of a model of remedial training that emphasizes the benefits of instruction by peers and positive community reinforcement for learners.

Despite the differences in approach at the provincial level, efforts do exist to co-ordinate actions to a certain degree among provinces and to share information about successful programs. The Council of Ministers of Education disseminates information about literacy programs in the various provinces. The Atlantic and the Western provinces have also collaborated in planning within their regions. However, provincial autonomy remains the rule, and co-ordination of programs is made more difficult by the fact that different provincial ministries (and often several departments or ministries within each province) are responsible for literacy. Further, just as bureaucratic reshuffling has been common in the United States, ministerial responsibility for literacy shifts frequently within provinces (as recently occurred in Ontario), introducing uncertainty about the continuity of existing programs.

In summary, then, Canada is similar to the United States in that both countries have had fairly weak federal participation in initiating, overseeing, and monitoring remedial programs. In Canada, though, the burden falls still more squarely on the provinces; the system has promoted innovation and at the same time seems to have created wide inconsistencies in the commitment to combatting illiteracy and in the way programs are run. As in the United States, there is considerable need for more consistent and objective evaluation of programs and administrative structures that will not appear to place provinces in competition with one another by placing the reputation of their education systems in jeopardy. Any international organization seeking to influence the direction of literacy policy in Canada should be prepared to work directly with policy-makers and providers at the provincial and community levels, in addition to relying on contacts through federal agencies.

Reconciling national guidelines with local autonomy: Adult education and adult literacy in Sweden

Sweden's adult education system is undoubtedly one of the most comprehensive, and best organized, among OECD nations. In 1986, at least half the Swedish civilian labor force was involved in some kind of education or retraining, including both public- and private-sector programs. In contrast, 27 million U.S. workers, or slightly less than one-quarter of the 112 million civilian labor force, were counted as having participated in a minimum of one occurrence of organized training during 1984[7]. Only a small fraction of Swedish adult education, however, is specifically adult *literacy* training. At least until recently, the general perception in Sweden has been that illiteracy is not a significant problem except perhaps as it affects immigrants. It should be noted however that Sweden has recently set aside SKr 10 billion (approximately $2 billion) to be spent over 5 years as part of its "working life renewal fund" and to be used for structural adjustments of the labor force (more on this below). Presumably some of these monies will be used for remedial literacy and basic skills training even though, to the best of our knowledge, no funds have been specifically designated as such. Indeed, in a fairly recent paper on adult literacy in Sweden, Kenneth Abrahamsson provides some vivid examples of cases of needed remedial basic skills training[8]. At the Ortviken pulp and paper mill, for instance, a plant undergoing major technological upgrading, management and the trade union, with the help of professional trainers, identified 300 workers out of a total of 700 as needing retraining, including 75 to 125 with extensive basic skills needs. In another instance, that of a 4 500-employee car factory, a survey of approximately 1 500 of the workers identified 500 in need of "adult basic education". More broadly, the unions have estimated that during the first half of 1986, only 2 per cent of employees with less than nine years of schooling received more than one week of company-paid training, even though 25 per cent of the employees had spent less than nine years in school[9]. Still, whether or not literacy training is actually reaching the neediest workers, much can be learned from the Swedish experience since it offers, in contrast to the United States and Canada, an example of an adult education system that attempts to be comprehensive and that involves a high degree of co-ordination between local and national levels.

A unique feature of the Swedish system is that much of adult education is "popular education", supported by the State but administered independently. Popular forms include a network of "folk high schools". Another important type of popular education is represented by the "study group associations". These groups were formed early in the century by workers' associations and other interest groups, and they gradually came to be less closely associated with particular ideologies and interest groups. The eleven existing associations sponsor thousands of study circles. Although these groups are supported mainly by funds from the government and municipalities (participants also pay a small fee), subject matter and focus are determined independently by sponsoring associations. Courses consist on average of about 20 to 30 hours during about 10 meetings. Participating in the circles, which together accounted for 28.4 per cent of adult education in 1986, is a way of life for some segments of the population. In providing the network of folk high schools and study groups, Sweden goes beyond most other developed countries in making the opportunity for lifelong education a reality for its citizens.

Also unique to Sweden is a system promoted recently by the country's labor unions to make company-based training more widely accessible and more responsive to broad educational goals of workers. The unions pushed the government to establish "renewal funds" in which companies were forced to deposit 10 per cent of their profits for a single year, 1985 (or roughly SKr 10 billion), and then draw from these funds over a five-year period to pay for training, research, and development. Unions in the companies have a say in how these funds are used, and one general stipulation is that much of the money spent on training must go to basic training for those workers with little formal schooling. Recently, the unions have pushed for even more aggressive policies on company training that would guarantee workers with minimal formal schooling supplementary training.

A third distinctive feature of the Swedish system is the important role played by the municipalities in organizing adult education. The municipalities have considerable leeway in organizing programs but respond to a national policy with national standards and curriculum. The emphasis of the municipal programs is on serving adults who have not been able to complete secondary education and who may want to qualify for university entrance. In the 1970s, the municipal system was expanded to include a semi-autonomous organization providing adult literacy training (writing, reading, and mathematics). Still a fairly small part of the adult education system, literacy training has served mainly immigrants, who make up over half the students, and Swedes who have failed in school, are unemployed, or who have learning disabilities. It is fairly common for training for the latter group to be co-ordinated with other social agencies serving disadvantaged populations.

Some criticisms of the Swedish system of adult education include the observation that access is considerably greater for those with more years of initial schooling. In addition, observers point out that adult education in Sweden involves mostly part-time, intermittent study over long periods of time. While appropriate to certain kinds of educational enhancement courses, this model is not very effective in literacy training. Also, the system comprises a wide variety of types and levels of education, and the lack of systematic connections among the various programs may contribute to the low rate of progression from adult education into higher education. Finally, some observers have pointed out that even though the share of the population with less than nine years of schooling has decreased steadily, from 65 per cent in 1960 to about 23 per cent in 1986 and to a low projected rate of only 4 per cent in 2010, higher rates of participation in formal schooling disguise persistent inequities in educational content and student performance by group[10]. Adult education programs have not generally been structured to respond to these inequities. The "success" of the Swedish system, in fact, tends to be inferred from statistics such as grade level completion and participation rates in various programs rather than according to tight assessment standards.

Such observations aside, the Swedish experience still provides a useful contrast to that of the United States and Canada, countries which are still struggling to construct an administrative system that would allow simultaneously for local autonomy and adherence to national standards, and would eliminate some of the barriers that now exist among the branches of adult education. The more porous system in Sweden seems not only to accomplish these goals but also to permit active and direct participation of a wider set of interest groups, most notably those representing the interests of labor. Finally, the strong role played by forms of popular education seems to support those educators in the United States and Canada who advocate greater emphasis on learner-directed programs, peer instruction, and, more generally, the blurring of distinctions between "literacy" as traditionally taught and adult education more broadly defined.

Searching for an appropriate delivery model: The fight for literacy in France

In vivid contrast to Sweden, France has kept provision of literacy training quite separate from the rest of its education system. As we noted earlier, until the last decade, illiteracy was generally viewed as a problem of migrant workers. Even provisions for lifelong learning that resulted from talks between the government and industry, and extended to workers the right to take time off work to attend classes, led mainly to expansion of French-language instruction for immigrant workers. Numerous voluntary organizations, in addition, formed to offer language training for immigrants. The situation is summarized by one observer as follows:

"The voluntary organizations] are relatively recent, frequently partisan in origin, and after an initial phase of unsuccessfully seeking to undertake further political mobilization among migrants, have become pragmatic in their field of action and ability to negotiate government subsidies for their educational undertakings... It has been the custom, when looking at underachievement in schools or adult illiteracy, to note that it must be a 'migrant problem'. Consequently, an abundant body of research on the education of migrants' children and adult migrants exists with a wealth of comparative European experience. The same is not true for the need of adult nationals."[11]

Following the publication of the 1984 report to the Prime Minister on illiteracy, the government set up an Interministerial Committee to conduct research and co-ordinate efforts to combat illiteracy. The interministerial body, significantly, does not have its Secretariat in the Ministry of Education, which has remained somewhat aloof from the group's efforts and from policy regarding literacy in general. The effect is to perpetuate a system in which initiatives on literacy remain fragmented, divided among various agencies that serve different segments of the population with high educational needs. The interministerial group is poorly funded and cannot itself sponsor major new programs. The group does try to help co-ordinate literacy policy in different parts of the country through regional representation, but without the ability to either extend or withhold funding, the coherence between national and local level policy remains weak.

The relative weakness of the literacy campaign in France may reflect simply a lack of strong commitment[12]. Potentially powerful vehicles for addressing the problem are already in place but remain underutilized. This is the case, for example, with training credits available to unemployed workers. Still, for certain groups of these workers, the system of training credit is now being extended to offer up to 1 100 hours worth of retraining rather than the standard 450 hours. Also, the Interministerial Committee is looking into ways in which to redirect minimum annual training monies set aside by French firms under the law to efforts promoting literacy and basic skill training. Additionally, the Interministerial Committee is pushing for the creation of a system of "individualized training credits" (*crédit-formation individualisé*) for school drop-outs or school-deficient youths that would allow them to collect up to 1 600 hours of remedial training over a period of several years.

The United Kingdom's "bottom-up" literacy movement

It is useful to take a brief look at literacy campaigns in the United Kingdom since they present yet another distinctive pattern of policy and training. In contrast to both France and Sweden, which emphasize strongly the use of professional trainers in adult education and literacy programs, the United Kingdom has until relatively recently built its literacy campaign upon the efforts of voluntary organizations. The vocal demands of community-based workers in the British Association of Settlements helped to stimulate the creation of a three-year plan for a national literacy campaign between 1975 and 1978. Key to the plan was the participation of the BBC in advertising to recruit both learners and volunteer instructors. The government also announced funding of £1 million per year to be disbursed to local literacy programs, and a co-ordinating body was formed to oversee the campaign. The response went considerably beyond initial expectations. The three-year campaign attracted 155 000 adult learners. After initially targeting male, working-class learners with very limited abilities, the BBC broadened its approach to try to attract a more diverse group of learners with a wider mix of skills.

After the first three years, the campaign underwent some significant changes. The national advertising and recruitment effort ended, and responsibility for co-ordination was shifted to a new and smaller body, the Adult Literacy and Basic Skills Unit. With considerably less funding, and a budget that was subject to year-by-year renewal, the unit switched the emphasis to local responsibility for recruitment of students and volunteers. Not surprisingly, the number of learners coming forward each year decreased. In the broader political context of budget cuts in education, and uncertainty about the fate of existing programs, links could not be established between various programs serving underskilled populations. Difficulties stemming from the heavy reliance on volunteers – the need for better instructor training and more program continuity, for example – have not been addressed given the dearth of funds.

The initial stages of the 1970s literacy campaign suggested a successful model for combining strong state action, media participation, and community support. But the fate of the campaign following the start-up period warns of some of the dangers of attempting a facile switch in responsibility from the national to the local level without providing sufficient funding or infrastructure to ensure program continuity. At the same time, this experience highlights the importance of strong community participation as perhaps a necessary, though not sufficient, condition for successful implementation of national policy.

But in recent years, recognizing both benefits and limitations of the policy pursued in the early 1980s, the central government has been providing stronger financial and programmatic support to the Adult Literacy and Basic Skill Unit's activities, while preserving the local orientation.

Awaiting national awareness: The Federal Republic of Germany[13]

Germany's high rate of economic growth and its long tradition of compulsory schooling have together made public recognition of any literacy problem in the country slow to develop. Nevertheless, there are clear signs that such a problem does exist. The German Commission for UNESCO estimates that there are 500 000 to 3 million illiterates in Germany[14]. It is increasingly clear, too, that adults with poor literacy skills include many who have completed all compulsory years of schooling but who still find themselves unable to cope with the literacy demands of employment and civic participation.

Recognition of the problem began in the late 1970s, when a handful of adult education institutes also initiated literacy programs. Literacy instruction was an entirely new field in German adult education, which had previously focused on vocational training and general education. Over the next several years, and particularly between 1979 and 1982, increased publicity about illiteracy and the active backing of some state governments (for example, Lower Saxony and Northrhine-Westfalia) encouraged growing demand for these programs. The number of adult education institutes offering literacy instruction rose to 120 by 1982.

Steady expansion of the numbers of both courses and students characterized the remainder of the decade. After 1982, this expansion was supported and monitored by the German Adult Education Association's literacy project. The project conducted annual surveys of literacy programs at adult education institutes between 1982 and 1985, and found that the number of participants more than doubled during that time. By 1986, more than 6 000 learners were taking literacy courses in around 242 (or approximately one in three) adult education institutes[15].

Despite this clear indication of progress, a number of problems remain to be addressed in the German system. As in some of the other countries whose efforts we have profiled, the system of financing literacy programs creates some inequities. There has been no national funding of literacy provision. Each adult education institute funds its own programs, and institute budgets are in turn provided by the community. Not surprisingly, the commitment to providing training is uneven and does not necessarily reflect the level of need in various regions. In fact, the distribution of programs suggests that rural populations are being under-served, while the lack of a direct national assessment of the population makes it difficult to assess whether other groups who need attention may be difficult to reach through the network of institutes.

A further problem involves the content of literacy training. Although in 1985 about 80 per cent of the adult education institutes were co-operating with other organizations such as job centers and welfare offices, co-operation tended to focus on recruiting learners rather than revising the content of programs.

In the first years of rapid expansion, literacy programs have been largely separated from other types of training in vocational and basic skills. Recent calls for greater overlap between these types of training may result in significant changes; for now, the integration of objectives and methods, and the bridging of programs in institutes with training in other types of institutions, including the private sector, remain the major challenges in the German case.

Overview

This survey of national policy and remedial literacy programs in several OECD countries draws attention to some recurring themes. In every country the design and implementation of policy measures are strongly influenced by the nature of political links and tensions between national, regional, or local levels. In addition, the relationship of literacy initiatives to the existing institutional schooling and training framework varies substantially from one country to another and even among different regions in the same country. Both these variables, in turn, may affect the efficiency with which available funding can be used in a co-ordinated way to combat illiteracy and the degree to which standards of evaluation and accountability can be successfully applied. And yet, despite national and local differences, several common goals do emerge from our review of individual country efforts in literacy. Two are particularly worthy of note.

First, virtually all policy groups are struggling with the issues of evaluation and accountability. In the absence of performance assessment, planners are tempted to continue supporting existing programs while only tentatively funding other approaches that theory, political pressure, or a combination of both, appear to advocate. In fairness, however, program planners and policy-makers are usually ill-equipped to assess how well or poorly the new approaches may work, even though the shortcomings of the old approaches may be better understood.

Second, despite limited evaluation tools, policy is evolving towards favoring a multiplicity of delivery modes that include funding not only for mainstream institutions but also for work-based and community-based groups. In this respect, there seems to be a growing consensus among researchers and policy-makers that traditional literacy training and basic skills training should be brought together, both as a way of improving co-ordination of programs and as a means of maximizing the effectiveness of both types of training substantively and financially. Here too, however, policy-makers lack assessments of the effectiveness of different delivery modes, making their task of promoting the strongest possible institutional arrangements all the more difficult. In the next chapter, we turn to a discussion of alternative literacy efforts, particularly to those linking remedial literacy instruction to basic skills training and workplace performance.

NOTES AND REFERENCES

1. Larry Mikulecky, "Second Chance Basic Skills Education", paper prepared for the U.S. Department of Labor, Commission of Workforce Quality and Labor Market Efficiency, 1989; George Diehkoff, "An Appraisal of Adult Literacy Programs: Reading Between the Lines", *Journal of Reading,* April 1988, pp. 624-630.

2. Forrest Chisman, *Jump Start: The Federal Role in Adult Literacy* (Washington, D.C.: Southport Institute for Policy Analysis, 1989).

3. States have participated in both formal and informal projects for sharing information about literacy campaigns. The Council of State Policy and Planning Agencies recently sponsored meetings of policy teams from nine states and aided their attempts to develop detailed and integrated strategies on literacy; the report on their accomplishments has helped to disseminate information about literacy policy to other states. See Judith Chynoweth, *Enhancing Literacy for Jobs and Productivity* (Washington, D.C.: Council of State Policy and Planning Agencies, 1989).

4. Note that the term "college" in Frontier College does not refer to a college in the traditional sense of the term, that is, to a 2- or 4-year post-secondary academic institution.

5. Federal support for literacy training in adult education in fact diminished in the late 1970s. The early Adult Basic Education program of the federal government, the Basic Training for Skill Development program (BTSD), provided academic upgrading and general job skills for adults – with grade-level attainment from 0 to 12. The federal government purchased delivery of services from the provinces. An evaluation of BTSD in 1977 by the Canada Employment and Immigration Commission (CEIC) led to changes in the program that significantly reduced the emphasis on basic education and aimed to focus it more narrowly on employment preparation. Among the important changes was the decision to phase out entirely any academic training at low levels through this program; funding of training at 0 to 7 grade levels was thus entirely eliminated. For more on this shift and its implications for literacy training in the provinces, see Audrey Thomas, "Adult Illiteracy in Canada: A Challenge", Occasional Paper No. 42, Canadian Commision for UNESCO, Ottawa, 1983.

6. Numerous profiles of literacy policy in the various provinces exist that at least sketch their differences, even if they do not provide rigorous comparative evaluations. For general summaries of provincial strategies, see, for example, R. Darville, "Literacy Activities in the Western Provinces", paper prepared for the Department of The Secretary of State, November 1987, and "Prospects for Adult Literacy Policy in British Columbia", *Policy Explorations* (4)4, Centre for Policy Studies in Education, University of British Columbia, 1989, on the Western provinces; B. Perrin, "Literacy in Ontario: An Overview", report prepared for the National Literacy Secretariat, Department of the Secretary of State, November 1987, on literacy policies in Ontario; Serge Wagner, "Analphabétisme et alphabétisation au Canada français" (1987) on Quebec; and Audrey Thomas, "Adult Illiteracy in Canada: A Challenge" *op. cit.* (1983), J. Cairns, *Adult Illiteracy in Canada,* report prepared for the Council of Ministers of Education, February 1988, and the Provincial Literacy Secretariat, Prince Edward Island, "Provincial and Territorial government Support to Literacy Training: An Overview", November 1989.

7. Nevzer Stacey and Duc-Le To, "Adult Education and Training Markets", in *Skills, Wages and Productivity in the Service Sector,* Thierry Noyelle, ed. (Boulder, CO: Westview Press, 1990) Chapter 7.
8. Kenneth Abrahamsson, "Adult Literacy, Technology and Culture – Policies, Programs and Problems in Sweden", Swedish National Board of Education, 1988.
9. Anders Fransson and Staffan Larsson, "Who Takes the Second Chance? Implementing Education Equality in Adult Basic Education in a Swedish Context", Report No. 1989-02, Department of Education and Educational Research, Gothenburg University, 1989.
10. Swedish National Board of Education, "Swedish Adult Education Towards the 21st Century" (Stockholm: National Board of Education Series, 1988).
11. Leslie Limage, "Adult Literacy Policy in Industrialized Countries", in *National Literacy Campaigns,* eds. R. Arnove and H. Graff (Plenum Publishing, 1987), p. 305.
12. Leslie Limage, "Adult Literacy Policy and Provision in an Age of Austerity", *International Review of Education* 32 (1986); and *ibid.*
13. This section was written prior to the reunification of Germany and refers only to the experience of Western Germany.
14. Hans Schütze points out that if one assumes that about half of the 4.5 million foreigners living in Western Germany are likely to experience some functional literacy difficulties, as do a large number of Germans who have not completed high school (*Hauptschulabschluss*), the 3 million upper estimate given by the German Commission for UNESCO is likely to underestimate widely the size of Germany's population with some degree of functional literacy difficulties.
15. Elisabeth Fuchs-Brüninghoff, Wolfgang Kreft and Ulrike Kropp, *Functional Illiteracy and Literacy in Developed Countries: The Case of the Federal Republic of Germany* (Hamburg: UNESCO Institute for Education, 1986).

Chapter 5

LITERACY, PRODUCTIVITY, AND GROWTH: CONTEXTUAL REMEDIAL LITERACY TRAINING

It has become commonplace to refer to a number of broad trends in arguing that strong ties exist between literacy levels and productivity in the advanced economies. Most commonly, perhaps, observers note that the structure of these advanced economies is changing with the fast growth of the high technology and service sectors, and the relative decline of traditional manufacturing. New jobs requiring new mixes of skills are being created while unskilled industrial jobs are declining. Also significant is the trend towards greater participation in the labor force by women, minorities, migrants, and other groups which may have had less access to education and hence fewer skills but which are now growing as a share of the total workforce.

More broadly, the argument continues, firms have reorganized internally in response to the changed economic climate since the mid-1970s. In particular, increasing international competition and market diversification have led firms in all advanced economies to search for ways to reorder production so that they can respond more quickly and with greater flexibility to market shifts. One casualty of this change in strategy has been allegiance to traditional work structures. In industry, firms are seeking to reorganize production so that departments and sub-contractors may work together more closely and with greater responsiveness. For industrial workers, the changes often mean greater demands on them to be able to handle varied tasks, to respond to unexpected situations, to understand the relationship of various tasks inside the firm, and to communicate more readily both with other workers and with management[1].

The service sector has not been immune from a similar process of restructuring. Although considerable attention has focused on the creation of a large pool of low-skilled service jobs in the advanced economies, this trend represents only part of the story. In sectors as different as business services and retailing, we find that the organizational structure of firms has been altered to allow for more rapid product development, increased attention to customer/client service and sales, and greater reliance on proprietary technology as a means of producing a distinctive firm image. The implications for individual workers are vast. They tend to be called on to train more extensively in the use of special technologies, to deal more often and in more complex ways with clients, and to retrain more frequently as positions and departments change in function. As in manufacturing, these trends imply greater demand for communications skills and skills in retrieving and analyzing information in a more uncertain environment[2]. In short, then, in both sectors of the economy, many jobs have become more demanding.

The economic cost of illiteracy

The literature linking basic skills of the labor force to the competitiveness of individual firms and the economic performance of nations is large but relatively recent. In Canada, for example, the Hudson Institute has recently published a report on the skill needs of the Canadian labor force[3]. In the United States, the Department of Labor jointly with the American Society of Training and Development has recently completed a large-scale study of skill and training needs in the national economy[4]. This work followed an earlier study by the Hudson Institute, *Workforce 2000,* also commissioned by the U.S. Department of Labor[5]. A large number of similar studies is now available for most OECD countries.

However, almost all of the relatively new literature on basic skills is of a descriptive, prescriptive, and, mostly, qualitative nature, and little has been done so far to assess the *direct costs* of basic skill and literacy deficiencies on productivity and economic output.

A large and growing number of employers now recognize that deficient basic skills and functional illiteracy are a cost to their operations and that the problem is far more serious than they once believed. For example, in a recent survey of 600 senior managers representing a broad spectrum of Canadian industry, the Conference Board of Canada found that about one-third of businesses reported serious difficulties in areas such as the introduction of new technology, product quality, and productivity because of basic skills deficiencies in the labor force[6].

In addition to being limited, the available direct evidence describing the costs of basic skills and literacy deficiencies for business is often controversial because of methodological measurement issues. For the United States, Kozol estimated the direct cost of adult functional illiteracy on business at $20 billion in 1985, plus $237 billion in lifetime earnings forfeited by men aged 25-30 with less than high school level attainment. In Canada, the Canadian Business Task Force on Literacy estimated losses for Canadian business from known costs at C$ 4 billion annually in the late 1980s. Simply extrapolating from this figure to the United States, Mikulecky suggests that nearly $40 billion are lost annually by U.S. business as a result of illiteracy[7]. We have no way of knowing how near or wide of the mark such estimates fall.

Indirect quantitative evidence linking literacy to economic performance can be found in the work of economists relating skill levels of individual workers to both individual earnings and firm output. Typical studies involve measuring the gains of an increase in human capital, as measured by additional firm training or additional formal education, to the earnings of individual workers or the output of firms. Such measurement is indirect in that it does not measure the impact of the *lack* of skills on economic performance, but rather the impact of an *increase* in skills. In general, this literature tends to support the notion that higher skill levels translate into both higher individual earnings and higher firm productivity. Perhaps the most compelling aggregate evidence is that drawn from the work of economist Edward Denison suggesting that more than half of the productivity increases in the U.S. economy between 1929 and 1969 can be associated with on-the-job training and learning. More importantly, Denison shows that on-the-job training and learning during the period was twice as important as technology in boosting productivity[8].

While the relationship between skill level and productivity has existed for quite some time, as suggested by the work of Denison and others, the perception is that this relationship has intensified over the last decade or so because of the rapidly changing nature of work and skills under conditions of intense transformation in technology and in the nature of competition. Business groups' growing interest in basic skills and literacy training stems in part from this growing perception that functional illiteracy is a threat to advanced nations' competitive status in a more rapidly changing, and more competitive, international economy. And yet, as we noted in Chapter 1, despite the change in rhetoric, business commitment to basic skills and literacy training remains highly uneven. The reasons for hesitation vary. Some firms have been able to rely on other strategies – especially technological upgrading and more careful recruiting – to continue to manage the skill mix in their workforces. Others have devoted their energies to revamping in-house training in ways that address the problem obliquely[9]. Part of the blame, too, must lie with educators, many of whom have been slow to alter traditional approaches to literacy and basic skills training. Imported by firms that perceive a problem, many programs simply supply high school equivalency courses or basic literacy training that accomplishes little, both because the number of hours of instruction tends to be low and because the content is so far removed from workers' everyday experience that lessons are promptly forgotten[10].

It is clear, then, that both sides – pedagogy and work organization – need to be addressed if more effective practices are to be put in place. On one side, learning must be changed by altering both the content and the style to address workers' immediate and long-term needs, rather than to prepare workers to perform predetermined, specific tasks in the firm or to pursue goals established by educators. On the other side, work itself must be reorganized to maximize use of workers' new learned competencies, and to develop second-order competencies upon which additional training can be built. The growing recognition that the two efforts must be related has already led to the creation of some promising, innovative programs. While it is too early to evaluate their success in most cases, we can learn from surveying the key features of some apparently effective experiments in various countries.

Union participation

For what may seem obvious reasons, many firms in OECD Member countries have consistently opposed union participation in the planning and delivery of workplace training or literacy programs. Unions, for their part, have sometimes been wary of employer-sponsored education programs because they fear that work rules will be affected and promotions may be tied to members' performance. Evidence from ongoing experiments in union participation in workplace programs suggests, however, that these institutions may be uniquely positioned to address simultaneously the problems of work reorganization and enhancing learners' skills. Several examples illustrate the promise and also indicate the range of patterns through which union participation can occur.

Sweden is undoubtedly the country with the broadest union participation in literacy and workplace training. As we noted in Chapter 4, it was union pressure that led to the 1985 provisions requiring firms to set aside a portion of profits for a renewal fund partially dedicated to training. The unions had already established a strong tradition of participation in adult education. Two organizations founded by the unions – the Workers Education Association and the Educational Association of Salaried Employees – organize adult study circles that annually enroll about one million participants. Unions also influence adult education through the 20 labor-organized folk high schools and claim to include one out of six union members nationally in some sort of educational activity. While most of the activities of unions involving study circles and folk high schools occur away from the workplace and are not work-related, the trend has been towards more active involvement with workforce training since the 1970s, when the Swedish government passed measures aimed at democratizing work. Unions responded by backing programs to help train worker representatives, by encouraging study circles to focus on workplace culture and history, and by safeguarding provisions for paid educational leave[11].

Participation in the oversight of spending of the funds set aside in 1985 has given the unions their clearest opportunity to influence workplace training directly. Firms have generally resisted using part of the set-aside to fund adult programs for poorly educated workers, and such programs have been established only where unions have actively pushed for them. No evaluation is yet available of programs that have been set up using the renewal funds. One case that has received considerable attention, though, is the experience of a truck factory in Gothenburg, where 777 out of 4 220 employees had less than nine years of schooling. The union pressured to have the equivalent of $5 million of the renewal funds devoted to establishing low-level courses in Swedish, English, mathematics, and computer usage that were made available to employees during working hours and without loss of job benefits. In the first two-and-a-half years of the program, 230 employees participated, with a low drop-out rate of 10 per cent. Because students were drawn into the program by department, instruction could be tailored somewhat to include material from the workplace. Absenteeism in participating departments apparently went down during the program, and production rates were held constant despite the time away from work devoted to study[12].

Despite the strong tradition of union participation in adult education, initiatives such as the one at Gothenburg mark a departure from the past because they necessitate direct involvement in education at the workplace. Continuing this trend may be necessary to the goal of truly democratizing the Swedish workplace[13]. In particular, such workplace programs may be able to reach a population – poorly educated Swedish-born adults – who has not participated in large numbers in the municipal adult education system, where most literacy training has been located until now.

A second, quite different type of union participation is that found in the U.S. automobile industry since the early 1980s. In 1982 Ford and the United Auto Workers (UAW) agreed to establish a jointly-run program to assist workers with education and training. Similar agreements were subsequently reached between the UAW and the two other major automobile makers, Chrysler and General Motors. The organizations are unique in that they are entirely co-managed by company and union representatives. They are also richly funded, drawing off a "tax" based on the total number of employee hours worked.

The UAW-GM Human Resources Center, founded in 1984, now claims the title of the largest privately-funded education center in the world, serving 400 000 UAW-represented GM employees distributed in 147 plants. Programs that the center supports (on a $150-200 million annual budget, representing 19 cents per hour worked, or about $400 for each of 320 000 active workers) include health and safety education, job-related skill development, tuition assistance, pre-retirement planning, and training and job placement for displaced workers. The organization operates 12 centers located near GM plants throughout the eastern, southern, and midwestern United States.

Only a small portion of these programs involves basic skills or literacy training. But such training is, at least in theory, available to all eligible workers. Displaced workers applying for help with training and job placement are assessed in reading and mathematics. If their basic skills are found to be too low for them to benefit from either classroom or on-the-job training, they are referred to an outside provider for GED (high-school equivalent) courses or remedial instruction. Virtually all such instruction is performed by outside vendors. Similarly, most active workers who are shown to be in need of remedial training are referred to local schools for GED or other adult education courses. In the plants, problems with basic skills are more acute now than in the past because job classifications are undergoing change and workers must often retrain in order to qualify for newly defined, generally broader job classifications. The affected workers tend to be skilled tradesmen who have considerable seniority in the plants and who average between 40 and 45 years of age. They have been out of school for many years, and many have a negative attitude towards traditional forms of schooling.

Not surprisingly, the UAW-GM center has found that sending workers to traditionally structured adult education courses does not always respond well to either company or worker needs. Representatives of UAW-GM have recently worked with the Literacy Center at Central Michigan University to develop a grant from the U.S. Department of Education to create literacy training programs that are more sensitive to learners' backgrounds and more closely tied to their experience on the job. The plan is to set up pilot projects at several plants that will offer work-related, competency-based training centered around instruction using words, phrases, and tasks encountered at work. The hope is that the program will address the two most serious problems of the existing basic skills programs: *recruitment* of learners, given the clear stigma attached to training that is labelled "remedial", and *retention* of students in courses that reproduce the traditional classroom setting that many learners have already encountered and rejected. One component of the project will be teaching adult education instructors about work in the plants so that they can train other teachers to relate instruction to work experiences.

Michigan's project planners could look North for an example of a program that is already incorporating many of these ideas. Two years ago, the Ontario Federation of Labor received funding from the province of Ontario to establish workplace basic skills programs. The province's Ministry of Education had established a fund for such projects but found that few employers actually applied; the Federation of Labor was more than willing to play a major role in designing programs for unionized workplaces. The Basic Education for Skills Training program (BEST) is not just endorsed by the unions but is entirely under their direction. BEST currently runs some 100 groups with 6 to 12 people per group. In at least 80 per cent of the cases, companies agree to share some of the cost; workers attend the groups for four hours a week, two hours on company time and two on workers' unpaid time.

The BEST program, perhaps more than any other workplace program we have found, is structured to emphasize the linkage between learning and workplace experience. The program is not presented as one designed to address workers' 'deficiencies' or to improve their grade-level assessments. Organizers have found that in order to facilitate recruitment they must stress the fact that workers already possess valuable skills, including, in most cases, the ability to read and write at a low level. Classes are led by volunteers *from the workplace,* who are trained by program organizers. According to the program's directors, the success of the program to date rests partly on the ability of the union to recruit and retain learners by creating an atmosphere of trust and by informing other, non-participating workers about the project so that participants do not face ridicule from their peers. Whether or not this crucial feature can be maintained after two years, when the groups will be continued by the companies themselves, and without BEST funding, remains to be seen. Also, one criticism that has been raised against the BEST program is that little attention has been paid to the issue of how to help learners continue improving their skills after they have reached the limit of what the program can offer.

In summary, union participation has in some places allowed for precisely the type of experimentation in linking remedial education to work experience that many experts and business leaders have called for. Fears about unions using influence over training to challenge companies' prerogatives appear to be unfounded. On the contrary, goals that are difficult to achieve in workplace programs – high levels of recruitment and retention, relevance to work tasks, and reinforcement of supportive relationships at work – may be best pursued where worker representatives, and participants themselves, are closely involved in planning and running educational programs.

Curriculum reform

The examples described above point to a second area of change that is likely to alter the effectiveness of adult worker training. As we already noted, traditional curricula of adult programs, including most of those sold as "workplace literacy", consist of standard high school equivalency or remedial training that takes very little account of the backgrounds or occupations of learners. The trend appears now to be changing, as employers and learners are joining literacy experts in calling for more examples of customized curricula.

One noteworthy example is a project to develop literacy training materials for workers and trainees in the banking industry in the United States. The American Bankers Association commissioned a study of low-level jobs in banking for which some firms have noted difficulty in recruiting workers with sufficient skills[14]. The result was a profile of skill needs in various jobs that is now being used by a division of the publishing house Simon and Schuster to prepare customized basic skills training materials for the banking industry.

This sectoral approach generalizes a practice familiar in scattered, smaller programs where customized curricula are already in use. In the United States, the traditional separation between adult literacy and vocational education has in the past limited the adoption of such an approach (recall the example of the program in Mississippi that was discontinued because it did not meet the standards of the established vocational curriculum). Other scattered programs continue as quiet successes. In New York City, for example, the local government sponsors an expanding program to teach adult learners the skills they will need to enter publicly-funded nursing programs. A number of states, too, are working to set up collaborative cross-agency projects that will require customized curricula to meet the needs of particular target populations. And in a few sectors, business representatives are already working with local community colleges to create courses designed to meet the needs of technical personnel in their industries.

In Canada, the BEST program just described has made the fully customized curriculum the centerpiece of its program. No degree of standardization exists so that groups are free to use whatever materials seem best suited to their needs. Learners bring in the materials themselves and are encouraged to draw on texts from home and from their communities as well as from work. Frontier College, a federally funded institution devoted to basic education and literacy in Canada, has also partially adopted this approach. In addition to designing pilot programs that incorporate workplace tasks and materials into course work, Frontier College has developed a workshop to teach businesses how to set up programs using job-related materials. It is interesting to note that Frontier College has seen much more interest in establishing such programs in manufacturing firms and little demand from services. This experience may reflect differences in educational attainment of the labor force between manufacturing and service firms, with levels of literacy and basic skills performance lower in the former than the latter. But it may also reflect the tendency for services firms to develop their own customized forms of training in order to prepare workers at all levels to handle proprietary technology and procedures.

As the trend towards adopting customized curricula continues, we can expect to see the proliferation of two patterns. In one model, instructors will be trained to teach using any sorts of materials, and course content will respond entirely to circumstance and to learners' needs, as is already being done in the BEST program. In the other, educators will begin to develop materials that are customized for particular groups – technicians in a particular industry, for example. Many more cases already exist where this second strategy is in use. The difference in the future will be that such programs will no longer be classified as either vocational or remedial, but will combine both types of training in content as well as in funding. Distinctions will also become more blurred between the content of programs conducted in the workplace and in outside institutions. Adopting a customized curriculum is surely not a sufficient condition for success, but in combination with other changes it can apparently make a significant difference in program records of achievement.

Restructuring work as a training strategy

Just as classroom training must be related to work content in order to be effective, work itself must be made more responsive to training methods and needs. This has been demonstrated by both education researchers and business analysts. Research with military personnel has shown that when learners receive basic skills training and then continue in unrelated jobs, they retain less than half of what they have learned within eight weeks[15]. Business analysts point out that assigning workers narrow, repetitive tasks limits their abilities to learn new skills quickly and to respond to unexpected situations. Restructuring work, then, is critical to the goal of enhancing both workers' competencies and firm productivity.

This strategy has already been demonstrated to be effective in a handful of rapidly restructuring sectors where new competitive pressures have generated novel approaches to work organization. Some of these cases occur where decentralization of production has created a plethora of new small firms; traditional hierarchical relationships are broken down and replaced with more fluid work structures that allow workers to perform a wider mix of tasks, take part in some decisions about the organization of work, and even contribute to product design. Their experiences help to expand skill levels, which in turn support a flexible system of production based on fast response to rapidly shifting demand[16].

Although such systems of so-called flexible specialization have been best documented in the manufacturing sector and in countries where particular political conditions facilitate this transformation, similar principles linking skill levels to organizational restructuring also emerge in strikingly different settings. In some segments of the service sector, new competitive pressures have also led firms to restructure internally. As in manufacturing, one result has been to break apart and recombine traditionally separate departments so that such functions as product development, marketing, and customer service become more closely linked. Workers, as a consequence, are required regularly to perform a wider range of tasks and to make frequent decisions based on general principles of firm policy and procedure; they are also shifted more often from one section to another. Workers' encounters with "training" are not limited to the formal instruction they receive as new recruits. Instead, informal training is built into nearly every position and workers face retraining to perform new tasks regularly throughout their careers. Such systems for combining organizational and training goals are found even in advanced service industries such as investment banking and business services[17].

What significance do such examples hold for training workers in *basic* skills and literacy? The implication seems clear that building training into jobs will at least reinforce other types of learning, even if this change cannot completely remove the need for complementary remedial programs. It is important to note, however, that simply adopting changes that make work appear more challenging, without actually altering the organizational context of work (and workers' perception of their place in that context), does not necessarily achieve the same purpose. Firms that have implemented task rotation or organized work teams may succeed in increasing productivity without enhancing workers' competencies; this criticism has been made, for example, of the GM-Toyota Fremont plant in California[18].

One clear conclusion is that much more research is needed to gauge the effects on literacy of various organizational structures and how they frame the content of work. This research needs to focus, also, not only on manufacturing, where much of the debate about restructuring has been centered, but also on the services, where employment creation is now greatest in the developed countries. Existing research suggests great promise in encouraging firms to seek ways to enhance skill levels through types of job restructuring that are also consistent with broader competitive strategies. Rather than satisfying themselves with blaming the school system, or workers themselves, for educational "deficiencies", business leaders must also critically assess the limits placed on workers' learning by the structure of work itself, and by the expectations firms hold for their employees.

Learner-centered strategies

Many of the successful and more innovative programs in the developing countries have not only abandoned more established teaching methods but have also advocated eliminating most fixed teaching methods in favor of a system that responds immediately to learners' needs. This is particularly true of a number of scattered community-based literacy programs. In adult education more broadly, the approach has been successfully used as a centerpiece of some larger programs, such as the adult study circles in Sweden.

Learner-centered strategies face an uphill battle within the literacy movement because they imply an ideology that legitimizes learners' authority to know their own needs and threatens the prerogatives of licensed educators to assess needs and goals independently. One community-based group in the United States that emphasizes a learner-based approach is PLAN Inc., in Washington, D.C. The program's director, Michael Fox, views with skepticism any claim that the content of literacy training can be apolitical. Every teaching method and textbook contains messages about learners' status and prospects, in most cases reaffirming their feelings of inadequacy and powerlessness. According to Fox, such feelings are reinforced when learners see so few immediate results from training. It takes at least one year of *intensive* instruction to raise reading levels substantially, and few learners stay with programs that long, particularly when they see paltry practical results. It is necessary, then, to address immediate needs. Examples of such actions at PLAN include helping students to vote – not by teaching them to read ballots but by instructing them about how to vote without knowing how to read – and coaching them to help them pass the drivers' test, if necessary by memorizing answers to test questions. If students see such concrete signs of change in their lives, the argument goes, they will be motivated to continue learning.

Once again, BEST in Ontario is the most notable example of a workplace program using a learner-centered approach. BEST peer instructors use materials that students bring to class, giving equal treatment to texts brought from home, from the community, or from work. Not focusing exclusively on work-related texts ironically appears to be an effective way to address problems with work tasks, since these are treated as part of a complex set of tasks that workers ordinarily face for which similar skills are needed.

Another type of learner-centered approach that is gaining prominence is found in intergenerational literacy programs. These respond to research findings showing that individuals' literacy rates correlate closely with mothers' educational background[19]. The programs use a wide array of pedagogical techniques, but all are learner-centered in the sense that they emphasize giving support to individual learners by affecting the environment around them – in this case, learners' primary relationships with parents or children[20]. The possibilities for applying such an approach in work-related programs has yet to be explored, but it is interesting to note that some studies of rapidly restructuring sectors show that dynamic growth is supported by inter-generational training taking place within family-run firms[21].

Overview

A major trend in adult remedial literacy training is the growing emphasis on training that is workplace contextual in nature. The shift to more contextual training has important implications for the active participation of workers themselves and/or of their unions, for the participation of learners, and for the transformation of curricula.

A first observation in closing this chapter is that while a number of experiments are now under way in several OECD countries linking directly literacy remedial training to workplace basic skills remedial training, it must be noted that most of these experiments have been undertaken by large firms with both the willingness *and* the financial and organizational resources to launch such programs. We must not forget, however, that most workers in industrialized nations are employed by small firms with very different levels of resources and commitment to remedial literacy. The implication is that emerging models of contextual remedial training that may work well in large organizational settings may not be appropriate to respond to the training needs of small employers. Very different structures may be needed to assist small firms in the retraining of their labor force. The terrain for experimentation would seem vast; so far, however, we have found little evidence of action on this front in any of the OECD countries.

A second closing observation regards programs emphasizing workplace-centered, contextually-oriented remedial literacy. Thus far, there has been little close scrutiny of their effectiveness. While there is casual evidence that some of these experiments are indeed succeeding where other, more traditional programs have failed, the lack of hard assessment may limit their diffusion as employers hesitate to venture away from traditional avenues.

NOTES AND REFERENCES

1. This argument has been stated as representing a general trend in the world economy. See Piore and Sabel, *The Second Industrial Divide* (New York: Basic Books, 1984). For a discussion of how this view applies to the shifting nature of jobs in U.S. industry, see Thomas Bailey, "Changes in the Nature and Structure of Work" (New York: Conservation of Human Resources, Columbia University, 1989).

2. See Lauren Benton et al., *Employee Training and U.S. Competitiveness: Lessons for the 1990s* (Boulder, CO: Westview Press, 1991).

3. Hudson Institute, *Workforce Literacy* (Montreal, November 1990).

4. See Anthony P. Carnevale, Leila J. Gainer, and Ann S. Meltzer, *Workplace Basics: The Essential Skills Employers Want* (San Francisco: Jossey-Bass Inc. Publishers, 1990); Anthony P. Carnevale, Leila J. Gainer and Eric Schulz, *Training the Technical Work Force* (San Francisco: Jossey-Bass Inc. Publishers, 1990); Anthony P. Carnevale, Leila J. Gainer and Janet Villet, *Training in America* (San Francisco: Jossey-Bass Inc. Publishers, 1990).

5. William B. Johnston and Arnold E. Packer, *Workforce 2000: Work and Workers for the Twenth-first Century* (Indianapolis: The Hudson Institute, June 1987).

6. Robert Des Lauriers, *The Impact of Employee Illiteracy on Canadian Business* (Ottawa: The Conference Board of Canada, August 1990).

7. Jonathan Kozol, *Illiterate America* (New Jersey: Anchor Press, 1985); Canadian Business Task Force on Literacy, *Measuring the Cost of Illiteracy in Canada* (Toronto: Canadian Business Task Force on Literacy, 1988); Larry Mikulecky, "Basic Skills Impediments to Communication between Management and Hourly Employees", *Management Communication Quarterly* (May 1990).

8. Edward Denison, *Accounting for United States Economic Growth* (Washington: Brookings Institution, 1988).

9. For example, by increasing use of contingent workers or even off-the-books workers so that lower wage costs compensate for lower productivity.

10. See Larry Mikulecky, "Basic Skills Impediments to Communication between Management and Hourly Employees", *op. cit.* (1990), for these and other criticisms of traditional workplace literacy training in the United States.

11. Norman Eiger, "Worker Education in Sweden: A Force for Extending Democratic Participation", *Scandinavian Review,* 76:1 (1988).

12. Anders Fransson and Staffan Larsson, "Who Takes a Second Chance? Implementing Education Equality in Adult Basic Education in a Swedish Context", report No. 1989-02, Department of Education and Educational Research, Gothenburg University, 1989.

13. Some research has shown that despite much talk about the benefits of enlarged jobs and greater participation in decision-making by workers, most Swedish employers continue to hold a narrow view of company-based training and to limit access unless specific, task-related goals can be identified. See Anders Fransson and Staffan Larsson, *ibid.*

14. American Bankers Association. *Survey on Basic Skills in Banking* (Washington, D.C.: American Bankers Association, Spring 1989).
15. Thomas Sticht, *Basic Skills in Defense* (Virginia: Human Resources Research Organization, 1982).
16. For more discussion of the relationship between flexible systems for production and worker learning, see Charles Sabel, *Work and Politics* (Cambridge University Press, 1982); Vittorio Capecchi, "The Informal Economy and the Development of Flexible Specialization in Emilia Romagna", in *The Informal Economy,* eds. Alejandro Portes, Manuel Castells and Lauren Benton (Baltimore: Johns Hopkins University Press, 1989); Lauren Benton, *Invisible Factories* (Albany, NY: SUNY Press, 1990); and Thomas Bailey, "Changes in the Nature of Work", *op. cit.* (1989).
17. See Lauren Benton *et al., Employee Training and U.S. Competitiveness, op. cit.* (1991).
18. On the effect of new management strategies at the GM-Toyota plant, see Mike Parker and Jane Slaughter, *Choosing Sides: Unions and the Team Concept* (Boston: South End Press, 1988).
19. Thomas Sticht and Barbara McDonald, *Making the Nation Smarter: The Intergenerational Transfer of Cognitive Ability* (San Diego: Applied Behavioral and Cognitive Sciences, Inc., 1989).
20. The Barbara Bush Foundation for Family Literacy. *First Teachers: A Family Literacy Handbook for Parents, Policy-Makers and Literacy Providers* (Washington, D.C.: Barbara Bush Foundation for Family Literacy, 1989).
21. See, for example, Vittorio Capecchi, "The Informal Economy and The Development of Flexible Specialization in Emilia Romagna", *op. cit.* (1989) and Lauren Benton, *Invisible Factories, op. cit.* (1990).

Chapter 6

CONCLUSION

A relatively new trend in today's literacy movement in industrialized nations is to emphasize the role that the community and the workplace can play as settings for the remedial education of adults. This trend implies a challenge to established education systems, including institutions devoted solely to adult education. Some countries already possess a strong tradition of adult education supported by community organizations and interest groups; this foundation should help to support coalitions to provide workplace training that pursues not only company objectives but also the broad educational goals of workers. In Sweden, for example, strong past union participation in adult education in community settings is leading, logically, to union involvement in workplace programs, while a long tradition of participation by a large spectrum of the adult population in community-based training programs is preparing individuals for a more active role in remedial training programs based at work.

In most countries, however, the tradition of remedial adult education is weaker, its linkage with work is not well developed, and considerable barriers remain to the development of effective workplace, or, at least, work-oriented literacy training. In the United States, where low levels of literacy in the adult population are perhaps most explicitly related to economic performance concerns, state agencies are struggling to establish new approaches to the problem that cut across entrenched institutional interests. Still, advances seem slow in comparison to needs. Even well-funded joint union-company, work-oriented remedial basic skills programs are able to move only very slowly towards integrating literacy into traditional workplace training. In Germany and France, the isolation of literacy programs from school-based education (in Germany, in adult education institutes and in France, in programs serving populations with special needs) places other kinds of limits on the scope for alliances among educators, firms, and learners in fomenting effective remedial programs.

Still, the similarities in program trends among the countries studied appear most striking. It seems evident that common economic pressures are driving actions on literacy in the industrialized nations. The concern is for maintaining growth in a more competitive and more technologically complex environment in part by fostering organizational flexibility and innovation, properties that are rightly perceived to be a function of the workforce's capacities for learning and on-the-job co-operation. These pressures call for more basic skills training in the workplace, more integration of work-related and non-work-related content, more support for participatory organizational models in both work and training, and closer ties to community organizations and other local interest groups. Some of the similarities in program trends among industrialized nations may derive also from a climate of public-sector fiscal austerity. In a number of cases, calls for more workplace programs and greater community participation in literacy training respond directly to the relative decline of public funding for traditional educational institutions. Thus, the trends we outline follow a double logic: a push for the delivery of more varied and more effective educational programs and the pull to fill widening gaps in the delivery system as established providers become more fiscally and politically constrained.

The task of clarifying these trends and identifying successful resolutions to the dilemmas they raise must rest on a solid understanding of the issues at hand. In that respect, our discussion has pointed towards several areas in which considerably more research is needed. First, much more attention should be devoted to evaluations and assessments of the content and nature of existing programs. While our understanding of the literacy needs may have improved, we still know too little about the best teaching methods for meeting literacy goals. Too little is known about the effectiveness of individual programs as measured by retention rates of participants, skill improvement of participants, or similarly relevant measures.

Second, more analysis of institutional arrangements that support or deter effective program leadership and management would be useful. As we have emphasized, similar goals are being pursued in a wide range of institutional-administrative settings, with varying success. Although certain political and bureaucratic constraints cannot be easily altered, policy-makers may learn a great deal from the study of alternative administrative arrangements that are being used to frame new literacy efforts in other countries and in other local polities. Business leaders, too, would benefit from examining case studies of effective alliances among government, business, educators, and learners in promoting literacy training and broad-based worker education. We also need to know more about the cost effectiveness of various programs. The dearth of knowledge about the performance rate of particular programs and the effectiveness of various institutional arrangements is hindering policy-makers – in government, business, unions, community organizations, or schools – in identifying and diffusing the most effective programs. The result is a tendency by all to overly rely on traditional programs and shy away from program innovation.

Third, an equally strong case can be made that countries that have yet to conduct a national assessment of the illiteracy problem should do so. As the U.S., Canadian, and French examples indicate, national assessments can be particularly useful in raising national consciousness about the issue, in identifying target populations, and, in turn, in assessing needed resources and optimal delivery modes. The issue is sufficiently important to warrant additional discussion. In the following two annexes we review a range of alternatives for carrying out quantitative assessments of the literacy needs of industrialized nations. We urge readers to give those annexes at least as much attention as they have given to this report.

Finally, as part of a broad assessment of the literacy needs of individual countries, there is a need for a much sharper assessment of the costs of illiteracy to individual firms and to the aggregate economy. Of particular interest would be to understand whether the cost of illiteracy falls evenly across the economy or, instead, is borne disproportionately by certain firms and institutions as defined, for example, by size or by sector. For instance, if it is the case that small firms are characterized by a larger share of their workers with poor basic and literacy skills, then the issue of how to provide remedial training to workers employed in small firms deserves special attention. As we have noted earlier, most innovation in workplace-oriented remedial literacy and basic skills programs has taken place in large organizations. It is far from clear, however, that such programs can be transferred wholesale to the rest of the economy. Only more analysis and more experimentation can ultimately help us in this area.

Annex 1

CANADA'S SURVEY OF LITERACY SKILLS USED IN DAILY ACTIVITIES[1]:
SURVEY PREPARATION AND MEASUREMENT ISSUES

Alvin Satin, Karen Kelly and Gilles Montigny, Statistics Canada

Stan Jones, Carleton University

Background

Literacy has long been recognized as essential for those who wish to function effectively in countries such as Canada where the use of printed materials has become so pervasive. Literacy provides the means to acquire knowledge of the world and to communicate with others.

Recent reports have raised literacy as an important national issue. These reports have brought to light both the extent of the problem of low literacy skill levels among segments of the Canadian population and the attendant costs to business and society. Other studies have stressed the literacy requirements of a changing workforce operating within an increasingly competitive global market[2].

In response to the need for an accurate in-depth study of literacy in Canada, a national literacy assessment was undertaken by Statistics Canada in 1989. The objectives and methodology of the survey are described in the sections which follow.

Survey objectives and data requirements of Canada's Survey of Literacy Skills Used in Daily Activities (LSUDA)

The primary objective of the study was to develop a data base which, upon analysis, would lead to a better understanding of the literacy skills of the Canadian population and hence afford enhanced opportunities for program planning and targeting of clientele. More specifically, the major objectives of the survey were:

1. To provide a direct assessment of *reading, writing,* and *numeracy* skills of the Canadian adult population;
2. To identify groups in Canadian society whose literacy skill levels place them at high risk; and
3. To establish the linkages between assessed literacy levels and other socio-economic variables.

The principal data requirements of the Survey of Literacy Skills Used in Daily Activities (LSUDA) were thus to provide a statistically reliable overall profile of the literacy skills of the population in Canada, its regions and provinces. Secondary requirements for the survey were to examine these profiles within groups classified by socio-economic and background variables such as age and educational attainment with particular emphasis on high risk categories (persons with low educational attainment and young adults).

Conceptualizing literacy

Statistics Canada's definition of literacy (see Chapter 3 above) takes off from UNESCO's 1978 definition. The 1978 UNESCO "Revised Recommendation Concerning the International Standardization of Educational Statistics" provided the following definition of functional literacy:

"A person is *functionally literate* who can engage in all those activities in which literacy is required for effective functioning of his/her group and community and also for enabling him/her to continue to use reading, writing and calculation for his/her own and the community's development."

Literacy proficiency is recognized to be "culture and time dependent" and, in this regard, is influenced by technological advancements which have tended to increase the literacy requirements that members of society face.

The task of developing a literacy definition for Canada is particularly difficult because of the multicultural nature of its society. To develop a measure of literacy unique to each Canadian sub-culture would be to leave behind the idea of a large-scale national survey, using direct standard measurement instruments. Yet, to ignore the literacy skills of various groups in various languages would oversimplify our understanding of literacy in Canada.

This dilemma of whether to develop a literacy measure for each sub-group, or to create a more standard tool, led to a decision to define literacy, in the present study, in terms of Canada's two official languages – either English or French.

To assess literacy skills directly in a multiplicity of non-official languages was deemed to be beyond the scope of this survey. Apart from the obvious operational difficulties involved in the development of equivalent measurement tools in different languages, to do so would have violated a basic principle underlying the design of the survey, viz. that it should restrict itself to the languages used by government to communicate with its population. Rather than a reflection of ethnocentricity, this strategy responds to the view that an absence of official language literacy effectively deprives a segment of the population from the benefit of government initiatives based on the printed word – in health promotion, labor market adjustment, or any other area of activity.

The skills underlying literacy cannot be separated from the "context" in which they must be applied. That is, the specific literacy skills individuals require in their everyday lives are largely dependent on their occupation, the activities they engage in at home, and their level of participation in community life. Hence, to put the skills involved in literacy into context, the three primary "domains" – work, home, and community – in which literacy skills must be applied were incorporated into our operational definition. Consideration given to these domains in the selection of measurement tasks ensured that a broad range of literacy demands that people commonly encountered in their everyday lives were included.

It was also recognized that the literacy skill that is required in a given situation depends on the type of material to which it must be applied. Thus, a third component of literacy, "materials", was built into the proposed framework of the LSUDA survey. To be specific, materials refer to the various forms or formats in which information is displayed. Following research by Kirsch and Jungeblut, the materials listed in Table A.1 were used in designing the survey[3].

Table A.1. **Materials used in daily activities**

Prose:	News story, editorial, text.
Documents:	Label, sign, directions, memo/letter, form, index/reference, notice, diagram/chart, graph, ad.
Numeracy:	Table, bill, deposit slip, catalogue order form.

Source: LSUDA.

The underlying framework for the survey thus recognizes the multifaceted nature of literacy and attempts to conceptualize it as the application of a set of information-processing skills to different materials or formats in their associated domains. While the survey does not address specialized skills such as computer literacy or literacy in the sciences or technology, it can be used to address the ability of persons to deal with materials frequently encountered in the workplace and thereby to indicate the degree to which minimum literacy requirements are satisfied for a broad range of jobs. The survey also establishes most of the groundwork necessary for conducting more focused research on literacy issues affecting particular segments of Canadian society.

Data collection instruments and methods

The LSUDA survey employed three questionnaires to profile the characteristics and the literacy skills of Canada's adult population:
- A set of "background" questions which gathered information on an individual's socio-demographic characteristics, on parental educational achievement, and on perceived literacy skills and needs;
- A "screening" questionnaire, involving seven simple tasks, designed to identify individuals with very limited literacy abilities (those who had very low literacy abilities were not asked to respond to the next questionnaire);
- A "main" questionnaire, comprising 37 tasks aimed at measuring specific reading, writing, and numeracy abilities.

To investigate how literacy skills were distributed within the Canadian population, the background questionnaire included such demographic and socio-economic variables as mother tongue, educational attainment, and income. Respondents were also asked to assess their reading and writing skills and indicate the types of programs that they believed could assist them at work or in their daily lives. (See Annex 2 for further discussion of the usefulness of some of these variables.)

The second and third components of the study involved the administration of simulation tasks using materials described in Table A.1. To be selected, tasks had to be of a type commonly encountered in daily living in Canada. The inclusion of tasks which were outside the experience of the majority of Canadians would have given an unfair advantage to those who had previously been exposed to a particular task. Thus, preference was given to tasks relatively free of technical jargon.

Another criterion guiding the selection of items was the suitability of administering such items within a household survey directed to the general adult population. For most respondents, participation in the survey was probably their first exposure to a test environment since leaving the formal school system. Coupled with the fact that it was the federal government doing the testing, it was necessary to limit the length and complexity of the items included in the test. Thus, reading aloud tasks or tasks more commonly encountered in academic settings were excluded.

Finally, it was necessary to ensure that the survey could be administered within a reasonable amount of time. This made it necessary to recognize the priority given to the measurement of reading skill levels and to restrict, in particular, the number of writing tasks given the relatively large amount of time needed to complete such tasks. Also, more items had to be selected at the lower and middle ranges of abilities in order to measure these levels with as much precision as possible given their importance in relation to program planning.

Many of the 44 items used in the test were drawn from the item pool used in the NAEP study[3]. These items were adapted to suit the Canadian context. Several new items were developed when their counterparts in the NAEP pool were deemed inappropriate for use in Canada. To facilitate the training of interviewers, the field administration, the processing of questionnaires, and the analysis of data, one instrument was developed in English and one in French.

The sample design used in the survey was determined in consideration of both the detailed data requirements and the need for face-to-face interviews to carry out a literacy assessment of the general population. Given both the large sample size required to satisfy the data requirements and the need to cluster this sample to reduce travel costs, the Labour Force Survey (LFS), Canada's largest continuing household survey, was used to structure the sample. Recent respondents to the LFS in the age range 16-69 were preselected on the basis of age and educational attainment to meet targeted allocations while limiting the selection to one person per household.

There were two separate administrations of the test items in the LSUDA. In April 1989, a pilot administration was conducted with some 1 500 individuals for the purpose of evaluating the test. Some minor adjustments to items were made, primarily to ensure a high level of consistency between the English and French versions.

The main administration of the survey was undertaken in October 1989 with a sample of 9 455 individuals by way of a personal interview conducted in the respondent's home. All tasks were administered to respondents in accordance with rigorous interviewer instructions. Interviewers were required to record, for each task, an attempt, a refusal, or a verbally expressed inability of the respondent to perform the task. Respondents were encouraged to look at and attempt all tasks.

LFS interviewers carried out the data collection. Their training was particularly oriented towards methods of administering the tasks in a neutral manner and adhering strictly to directives. The sensitive nature of the subject matter was stressed, and they were trained to deal with situations involving language difficulties, low literacy skill levels, reluctance, and other difficulties with might arise during the interview. Also, to promote quality and consistency in the assessment of test results, designated regional office staff were given special training to score the answers in a centralized manner. The response rate for the October 1989 survey was 70 per cent.

The functional literacy continuum

It is generally agreed that functional literacy skills do not fall neatly into categories but rather form a continuum[4]. It is possible, however, to identify points along this continuum that deserve particular attention because they are useful for program and educational planning. None of these points, however, divides the continuum into "literate" and "illiterate" because of the relative nature of functional literacy[5].

The table on page 25 above provides the definitions of levels used to describe the *reading* skills of Canada's adult population. Parallel definitions were developed for *writing* and *numeracy* skills.

What is crucial to note is that these four levels were developed prior to item development and served to guide that development. For example, reading level 2 items were designed to require only the ability to recognize and point out key words in a text. It was not assumed that all reading level 2 items would be equally easy or difficult; other factors that could not be measured, such as prior familiarity with the information in the text, would influence any individual's response. However, if a sufficient number of level 2 items were used in the assessment and an analysis procedure sensitive to the overall pattern of responses adopted, the effect of individual variation could be minimized.

The levels, then, are not points derived *post hoc* from the test data, but designed into the test. Thus the LSUDA results do not provide data to discover what the points/levels were, but data to confirm the model of functional literacy, reflected in the levels, that generated the test items.

Alternatives to the continuum

There are, of course, alternatives to the continuum notion. One could simply group individuals based on their correct responses to some small number of key items, a procedure used by the Adult Performance Level (APL) project in the United States and by the Southam Literacy Survey in Canada.

The difficulty with the key items notion is that literacy experts agree that no small number of items can define functional literacy. In a multicultural, multiliterate society such as Canada, it is impossible to say what literacy tasks everyone ought to be able to do. The APL approach has been widely criticized on these grounds (most effectively by Cervero) as has the Southam News project (especially by Fagan)[6].

Another alternative is to ignore individuals and report only on item performance as was done in early functional reading studies[7]. In this framework one would learn only, for example, that 65 per cent of the examinees could answer an item on reading a map, that 50 per cent could find a particular ad in the yellow pages, and that 71 per cent could circle the long distance charges on a phone bill. The usefulness of this approach is limited in that it does not lend itself to generalizing beyond the particular instance.

Because the key items and item-by-item approaches make it difficult to generalize to other literacy tasks and thus to program needs, they are less useful than the labelled continuum approach adopted by LSUDA.

Measuring functional literacy

Because the LSUDA approach identified certain points along the functional literacy continuum to use as markers, and created and administered test items to serve as tests for those points, it was possible to locate individuals along the continuum. This section addresses how the responses of the individuals tested were used to identify their functional literacy level.

Determining how to measure levels

Since it is the skills that underlie and generate the responses rather than the responses themselves that are of primary interest, a measurement system that directed its attention to these underlying skills was necessary. All tests are relatively indirect measures of the skills they are directed towards; all are estimates of some underlying or latent trait.

Further, it was necessary to relate the individuals' scores to the items that define the various levels. If it were possible to construct a perfect test, where the items were precise measures, it would be easy to relate individuals to levels; level 1 individuals would be unable to answer any level 2 items, level 2 individuals would answer all level 2 items, but no level 3 items. No one knows how to construct such tests, particularly tests of skills such as literacy. In the real world, level 2 people are likely to miss a few level 2 items and to answer correctly a few level 3 items. Each of the levels represents a range of abilities. The kind of scoring system that is needed is one that relates the pattern of performance on the test to the defining items.

Item response theory (IRT) provides an approach to measurement that defines an individual's ability in terms of the difficulty of test tasks which that individual can perform[8]. Based upon a regression model (a two-parameter logistic model was used in this study), IRT calculates for each item an estimate of its difficulty and an estimate of an individual's ability using the same numerical scale, commonly a scale that ranges from 0 to 500. An item difficulty is defined as the level of individual ability needed to have a certain chance of answering the item correctly; similarly, an individual's ability is defined as the level of difficulty of items which that individual has a certain chance of answering correctly. In the interests of applying a rigorous and realistic standard, that chance was set as 80 per cent in LSUDA, the same standard as that adopted in the U.S. 1986 Young Adult Literacy Study.

Checking reliability

Before the IRT procedures can be applied, it must first be determined that the test meets standard test criteria for reliability. The reliability for the reading scale items on LSUDA was 0.912, quite satisfactory for such a multi-item test. No single item had a major influence on the reliability.

Grouping items by difficulty

Once IRT difficulty scores for the items had been calculated, the ranges for each level could then be determined. Simply put, the items were ordered according to their difficulty score. The level for which each item was initially designed was compared with the groupings that emerged from the difficulty scores. In pilot trials not every item turned out to be in the expected level. Each item that did not group as expected was examined to determine whether the analysis of it had been wrong or whether the item needed to be revised. Only a few items needed revision, and this was largely because the French and English versions performed at different levels. Where this happened, an examination revealed significant differences in the phrasing or the presentation of the item in the two languages or in the text used in the different versions. These differences were corrected for the final instrument.

A cluster analysis program was also run to group the items by statistical similarity. This type of analysis uses several statistical tests to find the most natural groupings of the test items. The item groups, or clusters, derived from this analysis matched those from the theory-driven examination. The convergence of evidence for the levels strengthened confidence that they had been properly identified.

In summary, the following steps were followed to group the items by functional literacy level:

1. We calculated difficulty scores for each item using IRT;
2. We grouped the items by expected level and determined whether a grouping by difficulty scores fit the intended design;
3. We performed a statistical grouping procedure (cluster analysis) to verify the model-based procedure in step 2; and
4. Because steps 2 and 3 worked satisfactorily, the statistical ranges for each level were determined from the difficulty scores of items at that level.

The ranges for each level could be determined on the basis of the scores of the easiest item at that level and the most difficult item at the same level. This, of course, left small uncovered areas which were divided at even numbers so that finally:

Level 1: Under 160
Level 2: 160-204
Level 3: 205-244
Level 4: 245 and over

Determining an individual's level

At that point, it becomes relatively simple to determine a person's level. The individual's score is the item difficulty score of the most difficult item that the individual has an 80 per cent chance of answering correctly. In this manner, an individual whose score is less than 160 is at reading level 1; any individual whose score is over 205 but not over 245 is at reading level 3; etc. Under this approach the technical definition of each reading level for individuals is:

Level 1: Individuals who have a less than 80 per cent probability of answering an item with a difficulty of 160 or higher.
Level 2: Individuals who have at least an 80 per cent probability of answering an item with a difficulty of 160 and a less than 80 per cent probability of answering an item with a difficulty of 205.

Level 3: Individuals who have at least an 80 per cent probability of answering an item with a difficulty of 205 and a less than 80 per cent probability of answering an item with a difficulty of 245.

Level 4: Individuals who have at least an 80 per cent probability of answering an item with a difficulty of 245.

Because an individual's score is based on the total pattern of answers, not just on those of a particular level, it is possible, as noted above, that some level 2 individuals will answer some level 3 items, but they will not do so consistently. Thus, a person's level is the highest level at which she/he can perform consistently.

In general, of course, the levels are closely tied to the number of correct answers. For example, 98 per cent of the reading level 2 individuals answered fewer than 21 items and 97 per cent of the reading level 3 individuals answered 20 or more correctly. IRT scoring looks for overall consistency and discounts, but does not ignore, correct answers that are out of the pattern. In contrast, Simple Item Correct Scoring is more likely than IRT to reward an individual for a lucky guess and penalize an individual for a casual mistake. The ability to have some control over guessing and accidental errors is one of the advantages of IRT scoring procedures.

Conclusion

The evidence from the pilot study and from the main administration of the LSUDA indicates that the levels used in the study are identifiable points along the functional literacy continuum. It also indicates that the procedures used in assigning levels to individuals worked well. The national distribution of reading skills is presented in the following table. The findings themselves appear to be reasonable and that, too, provides assurance that the levels and procedures were appropriate.

Percent distribution of Canadian adults aged 16-69
by level of reading skills

Level	Percent distribution
1	7
2	9
3	22
4	62

More detailed breakdown of the survey results, by province and by socio-economic background, are available in other reports on the LSUDA project (see also Annex 2). They too confirm the reasonableness of the levels and procedures. Just how valuable the levels are, however, depends on the use of the results by literacy practitioners and on how they are used in analyses of the data by other researchers. We hope that the study presents new opportunities for a more focused examination of the issue of literacy in Canada.

NOTES AND REFERENCES

1. The authors would like to thank S. Murray, R. Porzuczek, F. McLeod, D. Dowd, N. Westran, D. Neice and T. Brecher for their comments on an earlier version of this annex.
2. *Southam News,*"Broken Words: Why Five Million Canadians are Illiterate" (1987); Canadian Business Task Force on Literacy, *Measuring the Costs of Illiteracy in Canada* (1988).
3. Irwin S. Kirsch and Ann Jungeblut, *Literacy Profiles of America's Young Adults,* National Assessment of Educational Progress (Princeton, NJ: Educational Testing Services, 1986).
4. Irwin S. Kirsch and John T. Guthrie, "The Concept and Measurement of Functional Literacy", *Reading Research Quarterly* (1981).
5. The concept underlying the development of a literacy scale can be found in Larry Mikulecky "Literacy Task Analysis: Defining and Measuring Occupational Literacy Demands", paper presented at the annual meeting of the American Educational Research Association, Chicago (March 1985); John T. Guthrie, "Locating information in documents: examination of a cognitive model", *Reading Research Quarterly,* 23, 178-199 (1988); John T. Guthrie and Irwin S. Kirsch, "Distinctions between reading comprehension and locating information in text", *Journal of Educational Psychology,* 79, 220-227 (1987).
6. Ronald M. Cervero, "Does the Texas Adult Performance Level Test Measure Functional Competence?", *Adult Education Quarterly,* 30, 152-165 (1980); and "Is a Common Definition of Adult Literacy Possible?", *Adult Education Quarterly,* 36, 50-54 (1985); William T. Fagan, "Literacy in Canada: A Critique of the Southam Report", *The Alberta Journal of Educational Research,* 34, 224-231 (1988); and "A Critical Look at Literacy", *Quill and Quire,* 55(2), 30 (February 1989).
7. Richard T. Murphy, *Adult Functional Reading Study, PR 73-48* (Princeton, NJ: Educational Testing Service, 1973); and *Adult Functional Reading Study, PR 75-2* (Princeton, NJ: Educational Testing Service, 1975).
8. R.K. Hambleton, "Principles and selected applications of Item Response Theory", in R.L. Linn (ed.), *Educational Measurement, 3rd Edition* (New York: American Council of Education, 1989), pp. 147-200.

Annex 2

DIRECT VERSUS PROXY MEASURES OF ADULT FUNCTIONAL LITERACY: A PRELIMINARY RE-EXAMINATION[1]

David Neice and Margaret Adsett,
with Wesley Rodney

The Department of the Secretary of State, Ottawa

Purpose

The purpose of this annex is to reassess the value of certain "proxy measures" of adult functional literacy in the light of new data from Statistics Canada's recent Survey of Literacy Skills Used in Daily Activities (LSUDA). The following practical questions underlie this inquiry:

1. Now that the results of Statistics Canada's direct skill assessments are available, what is the match or mismatch between these results, and traditional proxy measures of functional literacy? In particular, besides educational attainment, are there other "strong" correlates of adult functional literacy?
2. Can any of these "strong" correlates be combined to form a new, robust proxy index that might be utilized as an interim substitute for more extensive, but also more expensive, direct literacy assessment surveys? If so, what would be the risks and benefits of utilizing such a proxy index?
3. Finally, which is ultimately preferable, direct skill assessments or proxy measures?

This annex begins with a brief discussion of concepts and definitions and then moves on to a discussion of the history behind the use of proxy measures for estimating adult literacy and illiteracy. A discussion of the traditional inadequacy of proxies lays the ground for a short review of the most recent alternative: the direct skill assessment surveys such as those that have been done recently in North America. The direct assessment approach developed by Statistics Canada for the National Literacy Secretariat will be highlighted.

We then continue with a discussion of the empirical correlation between the results of Statistics Canada's adult literacy skills survey and various proxy measures, and we re-examine the potential adequacy of using proxy survey measures in the light of the new survey results. In conclusion, the strengths and weaknesses of the two approaches are discussed for both near- and long-term international comparisons.

Concepts

Our view is that the notion of literacy is best grasped not as a generalized concept but rather as a set of information processing skills which are accomplished, with varying success, within specific contexts and circumstances, and using particular materials or stimuli[2]. Ultimately, therefore, literacy is best underpinned by an *empirical* and *operational* definition. If people can perform certain adult reading tasks, they can be said to have reached a certain skill level; and if they can do more, they have a higher skill level, and so on. Adult literacy is, thus, best represented as a *continuum* of skill levels, each level increasing in complexity, but each requiring both decoding and decision skills related to specific contexts of functioning.

The virtues of an empirical and operational approach are many. First, the semantic tendency to exaggerate and juxtapose the two black and white categories of ''the literate'' and ''the illiterate'', while not entirely eliminated, is at least subdued. Second, the notion of a continuum of skill levels is a much better empirical reflection of adult functioning than is the old, rigid dichotomy. Third, this approach allows us to steer wide and clear of the ''conceptual'' debates about literacy, which, in our opinion, occupy much too much thought and energy that would be better devoted to establishing relevant empirical standards of adult functioning. And fourth, our operational approach lets us move back to the conceptual level with a very simple and elegant definition which speaks to the lives of adults – not in itself an insignificant accomplishment.

Thus, our current preferred definition is that offered by Statistics Canada where adult functional literacy refers to:

"The information processing skills necessary to use the *printed material* commonly encountered at work, at home, and in the community."[3]

The term ''information processing skills'' encompasses the three pillars of reading, writing, and numeracy abilities and includes both decoding and decision skills. These skills are empirically identifiable and refer to the individuals' abilities to utilize materials that are commonly encountered in work, at home, and in community life within the context of modern industrialized countries. This definition also carries the implicit sense that functional literacy is a requirement for full citizenship participation.

The use of proxy measures

In North America, the use of surrogate or proxy measures to estimate the literacy skills of the general population stems from two distinct traditions. One is rooted in self-report data gathered for many years by both the U.S. and Canadian Censuses. The second tradition derives from UNESCO's worldwide efforts to measure (and eradicate) illiteracy and from the application of this tradition to industrialized countries through the use of *grade attainment* as proxy measures. We will discuss each in turn.

For decades, the Censuses taken in North America have asked respondents to report whether they could both read and write a simple message. By that measure, as Stedman and Kaestle have noted, there was a tremendous reduction in illiteracy in the United States over the past century, from about 20 per cent in 1870 to less than 1 per cent in the 1970s[4]. The situation was quite similar for Canada, so much so, in fact, that the Canadian Census ceased collecting such information in 1931.

What can be made of these census measures? For someone to state, at the beginning of this century, that he or she could read or write a simple message was unlikely to refer to the same level of skill as that required today. Up to the end of the Second World War, the term "illiterate" was reserved for those with virtually no reading skills at all. One problem here is that self-reporting, at least when people are *directly* asked if they are able to read or write, is not very reliable. Those who do not read at all or who do not read well are quite likely to practice deception when questioned about their skills. And certainly, if the method of posing the questions is made in terms of a literate versus illiterate dichotomy, the emotionally charged character of these terms will skew the results. We return to this issue later when we look at other ways of tackling self-assessment.

What such self-assessment suggests, however, is that "basic" illiteracy, that is the inability to read and write anything at all, was most likely almost absent from North American societies by the mid-1900s, except for unusual instances resulting from extreme economic or congenital factors. Still, while people may have been literate, by the standards of 1900, would they have been functionally literate by the standards of today?

The UNESCO approach to proxy measures goes more or less to the heart of that question. In 1978, UNESCO issued guidelines to member states to collect data on adult illiteracy. Three approaches were suggested: *a)* a census question; *b)* special survey tests; and *c)* estimates based on school enrolment or educational attainment. The Canadian Commission for UNESCO in 1983 suggested, at least for Canada, that since direct measures of the number of basic and functional illiterates were not available, the percentage of adults with less than grade 5 could be used as a proxy indicator of "basic illiteracy"[5]. Similarly, the percentage of adults who had not completed grade 9 could be used as an indicator of "functional illiteracy". These educational attainment measures were seen, at the time, as satisfactory proxy measures, but they are now believed to be insufficient to describe the true extent of adult functional illiteracy.

The validity of the educational attainment measure as an indicator of functional literacy rests on two premises: most individuals who have completed at least the first level of schooling can meet the minimal expectations of their community; and most have reached a level of personal autonomy which is high enough that they can further improve their basic skills on their own. However, there is considerable disagreement in Canada as to the validity of grade 8 or 9 completion as an indicator of functional literacy. Some believe that it underestimates the magnitude of the problem, and that grade 10 completion would be more appropriate for Canada[6]. Others argue that it produces greatly inflated estimates of functional illiteracy since many persons with little formal education are nonetheless highly literate[7]. These debates point to some of the problems of functional literacy as a "relative" concept.

Nevertheless, educational attainment forms the basis for the various statistical comparisons and policy prescriptions generated by UNESCO. For many developing countries, any increase in the educational attainment of the population at large, particularly widespread completion of first level (primary or grade school), is seen as a progressive attack on the problem. For many industrialized nations, however, the picture is less clear since mass compulsory education at the first level makes comparisons less appropriate. Furthermore, and not to be dismissed lightly, is the thorny matter of standards for the basic literacy education that students are receiving while they are enrolled in the first level of schooling in some industrialized countries.

The question becomes simply this: are there individuals in industrialized societies who have the requisite *grade* level to be deemed literate, but who in reality lack the *skill* levels to be truly literate? The answer is unequivocally yes. When using grade attainment as our proxy of literacy, we end up *both* falsely labelling some as literate and falsely labelling others as illiterate[8]. With the results from direct skill assessment studies from several countries now in hand, the evidence is clear that while strong, the correlation between grade attainment and real-world literacy skills is less than perfect.

Direct assessment and the Statistics Canada Survey of Literacy Skills

In North America, the technology of direct literacy assessment surveys is now about 20 years old, going back to Lou Harris and Associates' 1971 Reading Difficulty Survey and the 1975 University of Texas APL Survey[9]. The most important surveys and their findings are reviewed in Chapter 3 of the main report. The outputs of these studies, while they embody important variations and nuances, essentially point to certain inescapable trends. Stedman and Kaestle summed up these trends in their exhaustive review of all literacy testing done in the United States over the past hundred years. They concluded that:

"It is reasonable to estimate that about 20 per cent of the adult population, or around 23.5 million people in the U.S., have serious difficulties with common reading tasks. Another 10 per cent or so are probably marginal in their functional literacy skills."[10]

Their summation is all the more interesting because it was made before most of the recent direct assessments had been done. The new results just reaffirm their estimates.

In the current climate, direct skill assessments are significantly better[11]. And certainly, when they are set beside the self-assessment results of earlier censuses, or the now tottering viability of educational attainment, they do offer tremendous precision, measurement accuracy, and indeed insight and clarity about the adult literacy issue. The technology of educational testing and sophisticated survey sampling methodology combine into a powerful strategy which allows countries to get hard numbers on adult functional illiteracy.

However, there is a certain cost for this kind of precision. These studies are labor and technology intensive. They rely on expertise in testing and survey methodology which is more developed in some countries than others. They also rely on an infrastructure of empirical social science research both for their guidance and ultimately for their acceptance by relevant authorities and trend setters, such as the media and elites. And with the expense must come an institutional commitment that better literacy statistics are needed and are worth the attention they will generate.

And so, it can be stated emphatically that, if cost is not critical, if the goal is to obtain the best available information, and if the institutional momentum exists to get there, direct skill assessment methods are definitely the answer. But suppose the climate is more tenuous, the resources fewer, and the national literacy momentum still in its infancy. Is there a possible path where better proxies might work as interim measures until direct measures can be acquired? We think so, as we will see shortly.

For the purpose of this annex, rather than trying to canvas the results and correlates of all of the various direct skill assessments that have been done so far, we will instead focus on the results of the most recent and also most detailed survey, namely, Statistics Canada's 1989 Survey of Literacy Skills Used in Daily Activities (LSUDA).

The Statistics Canada literacy study consisted of interviews administered to a representative sample of 9 455 persons aged 16 to 69 in their homes that involved a series of tasks designed to test reading, numeracy, and writing activities commonly encountered in daily life in Canada. The assessment was restricted to Canada's two official languages, English and French.

Skill levels were defined according to the abilities required to accomplish a variety of activities. For reading, the abilities ranged from locating a word or item in a document (for example, locating the expiry date on a driver's license) to more complex abilities involving the integration of information from various parts of a document (for example, reading a chart to determine if an employee is eligible for a particular benefit).

The survey employed three questionnaires:

  a) A "background" questionnaire aimed at gathering information on the individual's socio-demographic characteristics, parental educational achievement, as well as perceived literacy skills and needs;
  b) A "screening" questionnaire, involving a small number of simple tasks, designed to identify individuals with very limited literacy abilities (those demonstrating very low literacy abilities at the outcome of this survey questionnaire) were not asked to respond to the next questionnaire; and
  c) A "main" questionnaire, comprising the majority of the tests, aimed at measuring specific reading, writing, and numeracy abilities.

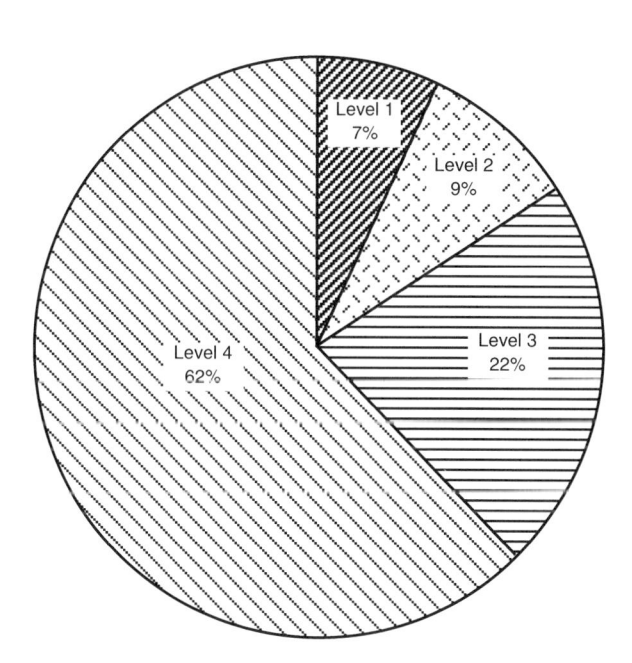

Figure 1: **Reading skill levels in Canada**
Adults aged 16 to 69

- Level 1: 7%
- Level 2: 9%
- Level 3: 22%
- Level 4: 62%

Source: LSUDA.

Figure 2: **Reading skill levels by province**

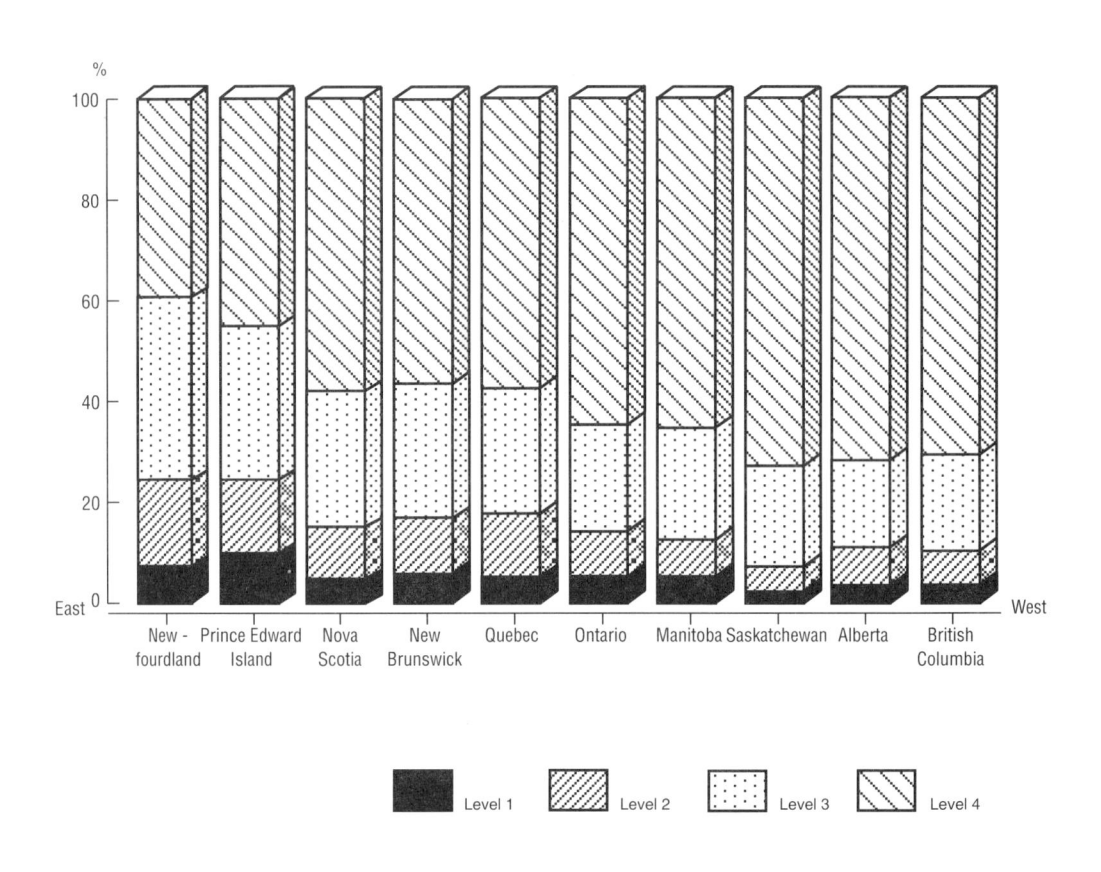

[Bar chart showing reading skill levels (Level 1, Level 2, Level 3, Level 4) for the provinces: Newfoundland, Prince Edward Island, Nova Scotia, New Brunswick, Quebec, Ontario, Manitoba, Saskatchewan, Alberta, British Columbia, arranged East to West.]

Source: LSUDA.

The main outcome of the survey was a separate test score for each respondent for reading, writing, and numeracy. To aid in the interpretation of these scores, respondents were arrayed among skill levels according to their performance on the test. In the case of reading, four levels were utilized as set out on page 25 above.

For the purposes of this analysis, Canadians at level 1 generally cannot read. Those at level 2 are described as having skills too limited to deal with most everyday reading demands. Canadians at level 4 have reading skills sufficient to meet everyday requirements, while those at level 3 have a reading proficiency enabling them to handle reading demands within a more limited range.

Figure 3: **Reading skill levels by age groups**

[Bar chart showing reading skill levels (Level 1, Level 2, Level 3, Level 4) by age groups: 16-24, 25-34, 35-44, 45-54, 55-69]

Level 1 | Level 2 | Level 3 | Level 4

Source: LSUDA.

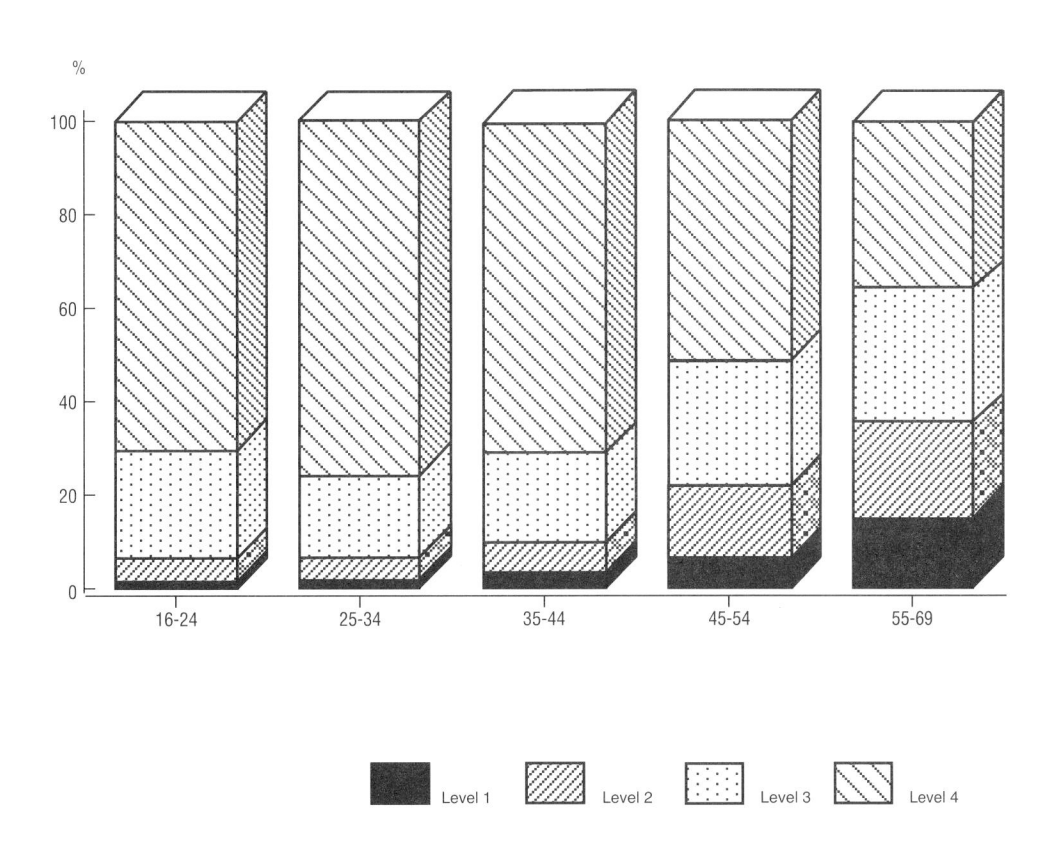

Figure 1 shows the distribution of Canadians across the four reading skill levels. Sixty-two per cent have reading skills deemed adequate for daily requirements (level 4) while 38 per cent do not (levels 1, 2 and 3 combined). Figure 2 provides an overview of the reading results by provinces. The figure suggests a smooth shift to stronger skills from the east to the west coast. While there has been much speculation as to why this pattern exists, no clear answers are yet available. We suggest that income levels may explain the variations as well as provincial age structures and the proportion of the foreign-born in different provinces, but other hypotheses are also possible.

Finally, Figure 3 provides a snapshot of reading skill levels by age groups. While it is clear that the population over 45 years of age has poorer reading skills, it is also evident that there is a large share of the Canadian population aged 16-24 with problems at level 2 and level 3 functioning. For young individuals, some of whom may have just left the school system, this is not an encouraging statistic.

LSUDA reading skill levels and educational attainment

We can now turn to the heart of our concerns, namely the quality of the relationship between the findings from direct assessment and those suggested by proxy measures of literacy. Figure 4 presents the relationship between reading skill levels and educational attainment based on the LSUDA results. The majority of Canadians with *no schooling* have level 1 reading skills

Figure 4: **Reading skill levels by educational attainment**

Level 1 Level 2 Level 3 Level 4

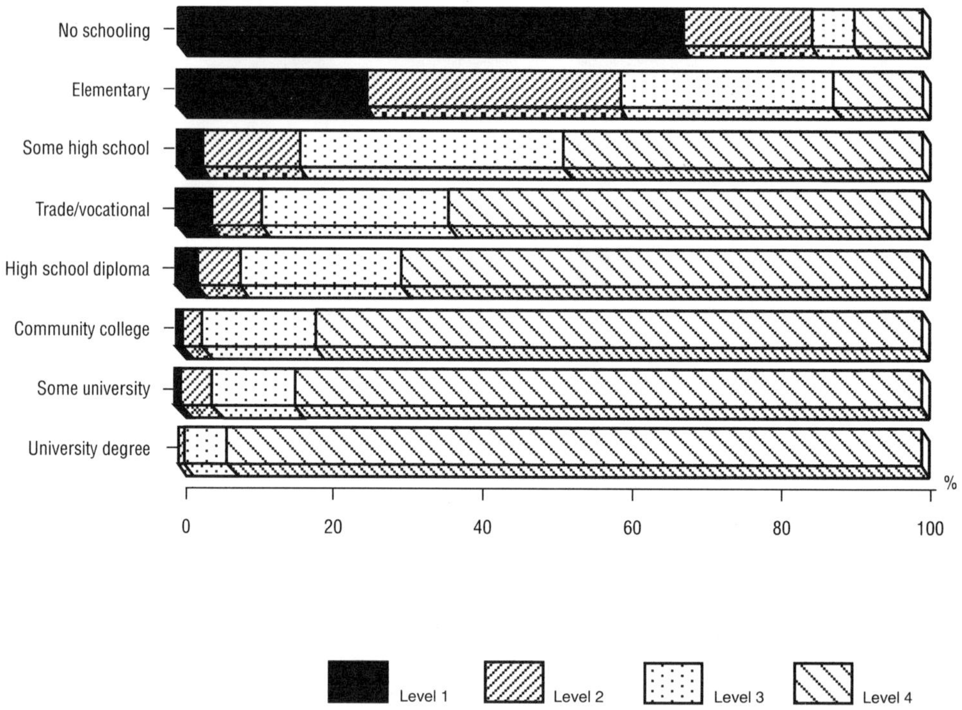

Source: LSUDA.

Figure 5: **Educational attainment and reading skill levels**

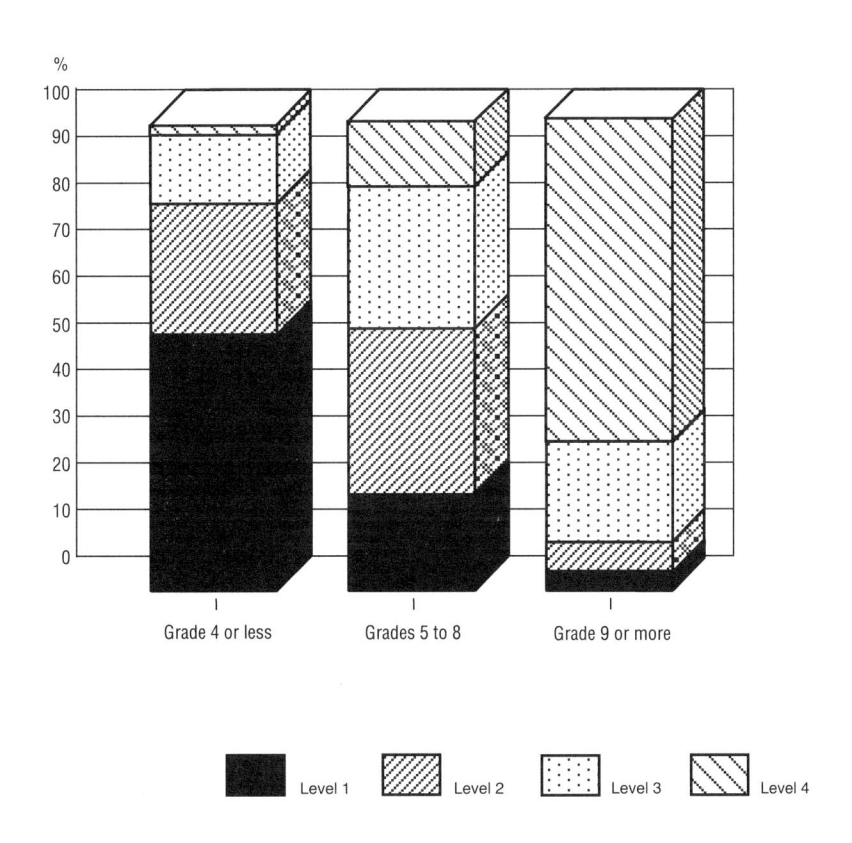

Source: LSUDA.

(68 per cent). Another 17 and 6 per cent of these people respectively have levels 2 and 3 reading skills. This leaves 9 per cent of those without schooling with level 4 reading skills. By classifying all of those with no schooling as "basic illiterates", the educational attainment measure would have falsely classified nearly one third of that group (32 per cent), those with reading levels ranging from 2 to 4. As for those with elementary (or first level) education, at least 12 per cent would have been falsely classified as "functionally illiterate" since this percentage actually has level 4 reading skills.

Figure 5 provides more insights into the adequacy of educational attainment as a surrogate measure of literacy[12]. In this diagram, education is grouped in the same way as it has been previously collapsed by researchers to measure literacy, with "grade 4 or less" used to indicate "basic illiteracy", "grades 5 to 8" to indicate "functional illiteracy", and "grade 9 or more" to indicate "literacy". When cross-classified with the LSUDA reading skill levels, the figure shows that as many as 44 per cent of those with grade 4 or less education would be misclassified as "basic illiterates" by the educational attainment measure. Likewise, up to 44 per cent of those with grade 5 to 8 education – with actual reading skill levels 3 and 4 – would be misclassified as "functional illiterates".

Things are not much better when we consider those with grade "9 or more" education. Using the traditional proxy, all of those with grade "9 or more" levels of education are assumed to be "functionally literate". Yet, according to Figure 5, as many as 31 per cent of those people would be falsely labelled as functional literates since this percentage actually has less than level 4 reading skills. The implication is that if we are to use education as a surrogate measure of literacy, a level of educational attainment markedly higher than grade 9 should likely be used as the cut-off point for functional literacy. In the case of Canada, Figure 4 suggests that "high school or more" should be used as a standard of educational attainment to assume "functional literacy".

Revising our educational cut-off point so that we assume adequate functional literacy skills at "grade 12 or above" would still make education the best proxy measure of literacy to date, despite its imperfections. The correlation between the LSUDA reading skill levels and educational attainment, as defined in Figure 4, is a strong 0.59 Gamma coefficient (an ordinal measure of association)[13]. However, there are other possible surrogate measures, such as self-assessment, which could be perfected or used in combination with education levels to produce an even more accurate proxy.

LSUDA reading skill levels and self-assessment of literacy skills

One question asked in the LSUDA survey was: "On a scale of 1 to 5, 1 being poor and 5 being excellent, how would you rate your reading and writing skills in English/French?". Figure 6 displays the answers to this question cross-tabulated with the respondents' actual reading scores, as determined through the test results. Seventy-two per cent of those who rated their literacy skills as "poor" had level 1 reading skills; only 3.5 per cent of them actually had level 4 reading skills. At the low end of the scale, therefore, self-assessment appears to be better than the traditional education surrogate which classified correctly as "basic illiterates" only 56 per cent of those with grade 4 or less education (Figure 5).

At the other end of the self-assessment scale, 76 per cent of people who rated their literacy skills as "excellent" had adequate reading skills (level 4), as did 70 per cent of people who rated their skills as "very good". These two points on the self-assessment scale appear to be as accurate, if not more accurate, than the education surrogate, which correctly labelled only 69 per cent of those with grade 9 or more education (Figure 5). Finally, about half of those who assessed their skills in the middle of the self-assessment scale ("good") had level 4 reading skills, a similar percentage to that of people with "some" high school education (Figure 4). These results suggest that educational attainment and self-assessment could between them produce a very strong combined proxy measure of literacy.

The ambiguous category on the self-assessment scale is for those who classify themselves as "fair". Test results are such that these people are distributed roughly equally across the four reading skill levels. Sixty-nine per cent of people who assessed their literacy skills as "fair"

Figure 6: **Reading skill levels by self-assessment of reading and writing skills**

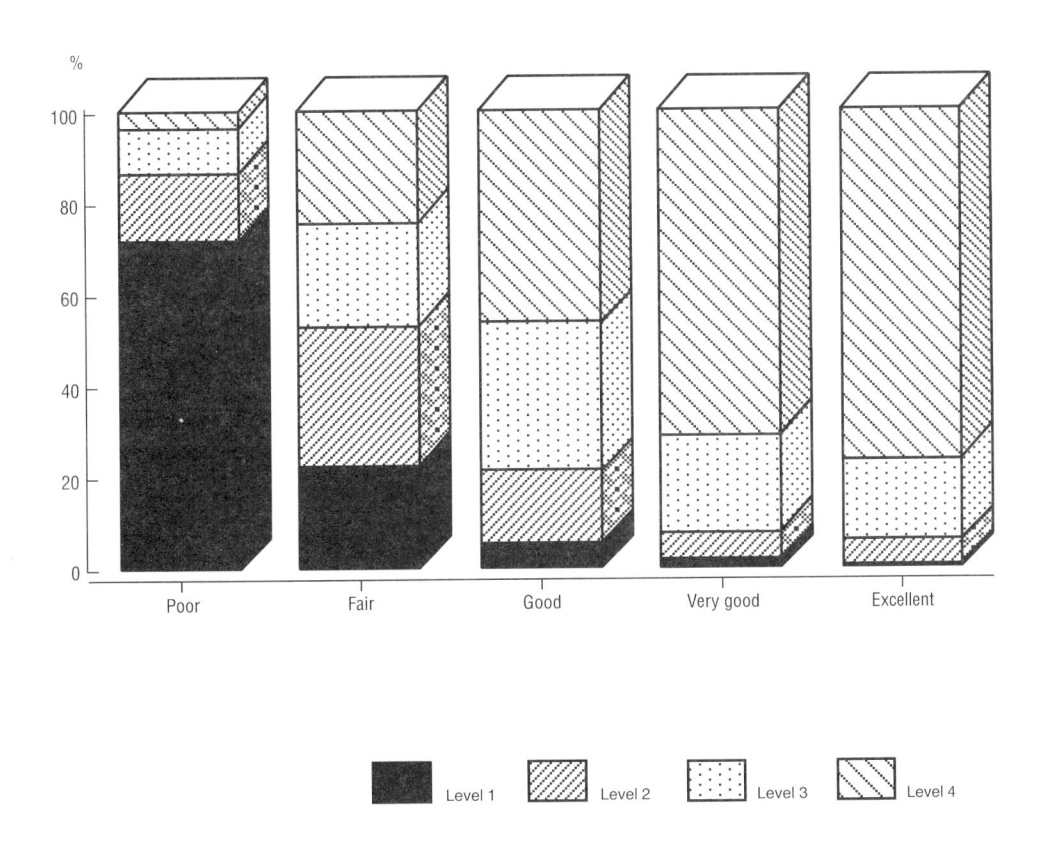

[Bar chart showing distribution of Level 1, Level 2, Level 3, and Level 4 reading skills across self-assessment categories: Poor, Fair, Good, Very good, Excellent]

Source: LSUDA.

have less than a high school diploma. This again suggests that a revised proxy using educational attainment – for example using high school diploma as a cut-off – in combination with self-assessment could produce an excellent indicator of adult functional literacy.

A Gamma coefficient of 0.46 for the correlation between self-assessment and the LSUDA reading skill levels indicates that, with further experimentation and refinement, self-assessment, either alone or in combination with other measures, could be used as an excellent surrogate measure of functional literacy skills. There is also a great deal of potential for subsequent refinement of the wording and phrasing of the self-assessment question and the response scale offered to improve the fit between the self-assessment measure and direct assessment measures.

LSUDA reading skill levels and frequency of reading

Another question asked in the LSUDA survey was how often respondents read newspapers, magazines or books. Figure 7 presents the answers to this question cross-classified with the LSUDA reading skill levels. While the relationship between frequency of reading and literacy scores is weaker than any of the others presented here (with a Gamma coefficient of 0.33), we would rank this measure next after self-assessment for reasons which will become evident shortly.

After the LSUDA data were collected, some preliminary research was commissioned on the development of a reading activity index[14]. Using a factor analysis of several data sets,

Figure 7: **Reading levels by frequency of reading newspapers, magazines or books**

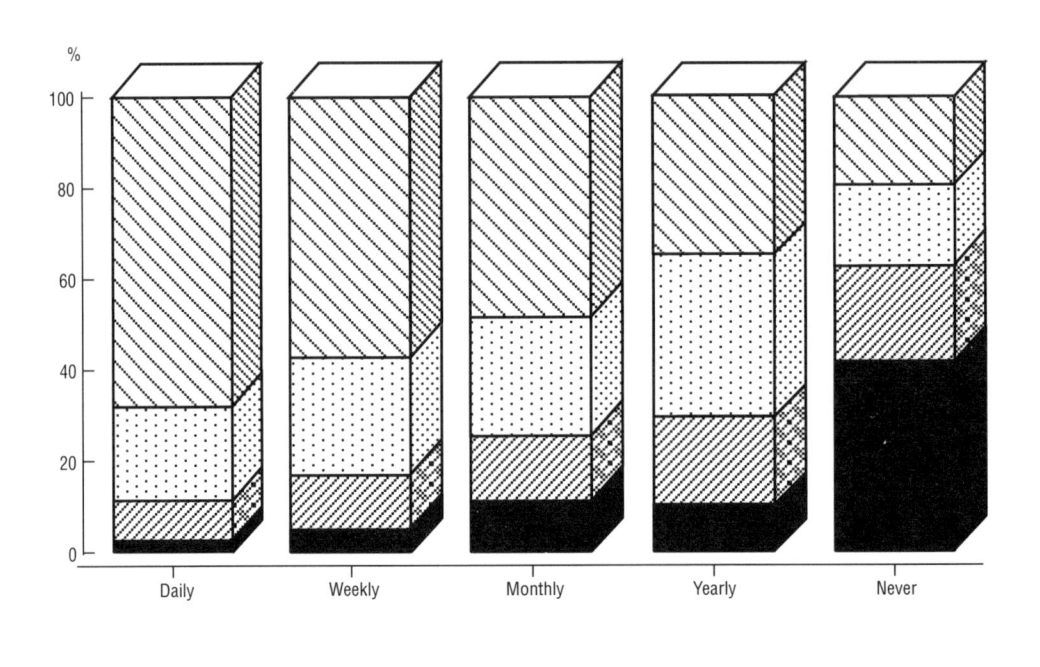

Source: LSUDA.

Figure 8: **Reading skill levels by frequency of library visits**

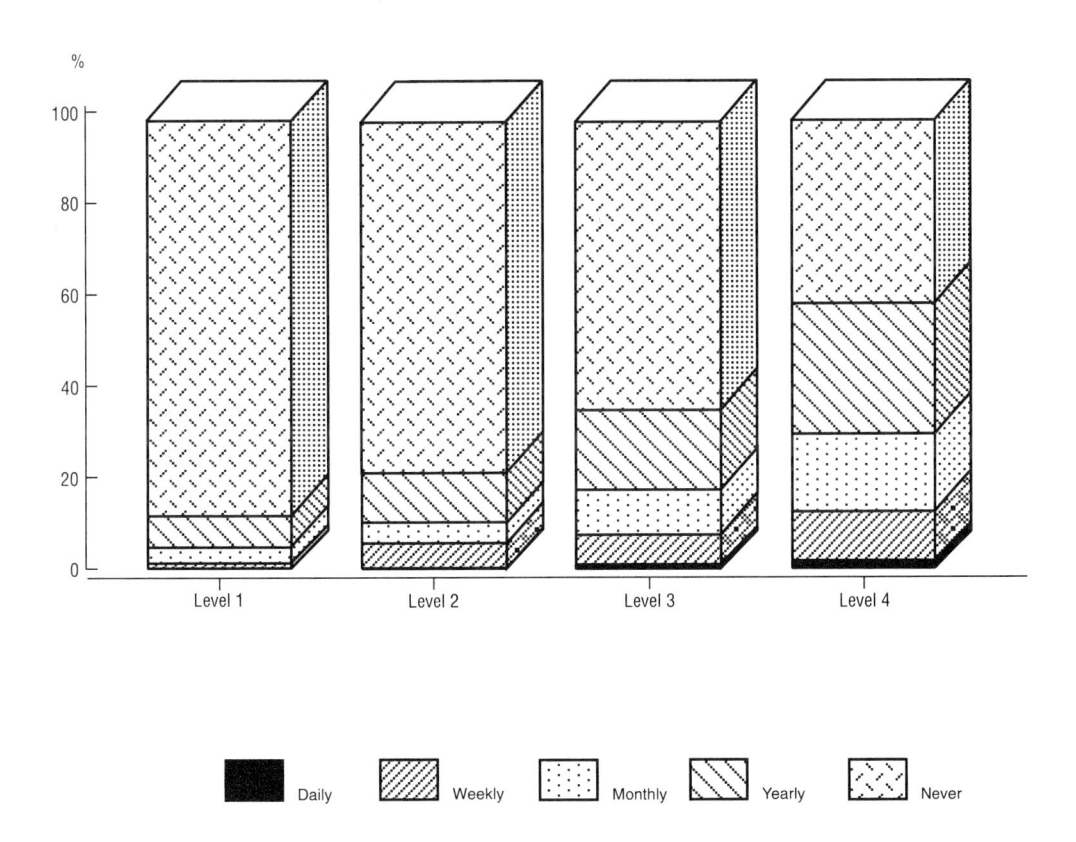

[Bar chart showing reading skill levels (Level 1 through Level 4) by frequency of library visits (Daily, Weekly, Monthly, Yearly, Never)]

Source: LSUDA.

including old ones, we learned that the frequency of *book* reading is potentially the single best indicator of functional literacy, perhaps even better than education. The frequency of *magazine* reading also loaded reasonably well in the factor analysis, though not better than education. In marked contrast, *newspaper* reading loaded very poorly. Regarding the latter, we learned that newspaper reading is much like television viewing and radio use. The LSUDA results confirm that for radio use and television viewing, everybody does it and does it often, regardless of literacy level, which explains why the correlation is weak. We have concluded that the reason why our measure of reading as depicted in Figure 7 is not associated more strongly with the LSUDA reading skill levels is that the correlation has been dampened by the inclusion of too many sources and types of reading materials in the LSUDA reading question, newspapers in particular. We believe that frequency of *book* reading is a potentially powerful surrogate measure of literacy. This potential is reflected in another correlation, namely that between the frequency of visits to the library (another question on the LSUDA survey) and reading skill levels (see Figure 8). The Gamma coefficient for this correlation is 0.46, the same as that for self-assessment.

LSUDA reading skill levels and self-assessment of adequacy of workplace literacy skills

In the LSUDA survey, following a set of questions on their present or last job, respondents were asked whether or not they thought their reading skills were adequate for that job. The specific question was: "Do you feel your reading skills in English/French are adequate for this job?".

Figure 9 presents the responses to this question cross-classified with reading scores, which have been collapsed for the sake of simplicity into inadequate skills (levels 1 to 3) and adequate skills (level 4). Only 30 per cent of those who self-reported that their reading skills were adequate for their job actually tested as inadequate in reading. On the other hand, 79 per cent of those who self-reported that their skills were inadequate for their job did in fact have inadequate reading skills.

Again, Canadian adults prove to have a good subjective self-understanding of the limits of their reading skill levels. And again, the LSUDA survey suggests another strong proxy measure that could be used for measuring literacy, particularly workforce literacy.

Figure 9: **Reading levels by whether reading skills considered adequate for job**

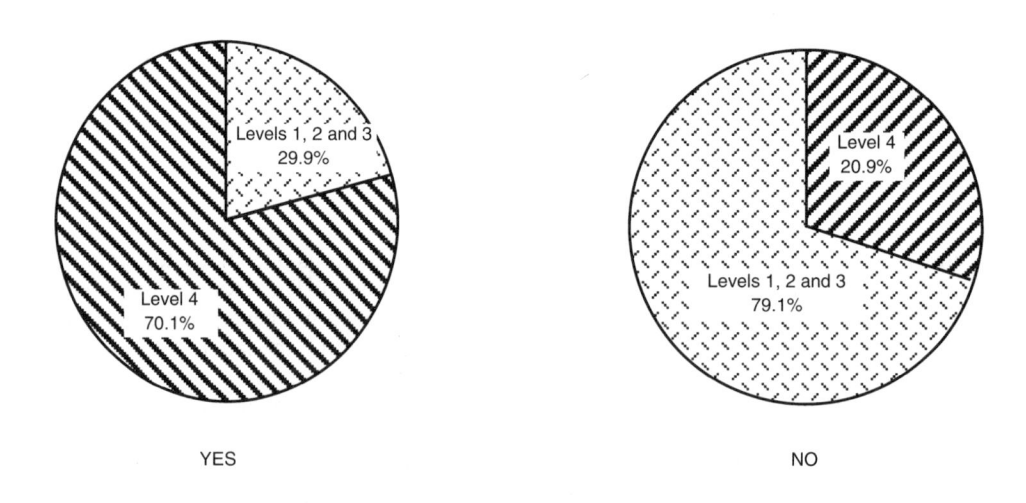

YES
- Levels 1, 2 and 3: 29.9%
- Level 4: 70.1%

NO
- Level 4: 20.9%
- Levels 1, 2 and 3: 79.1%

Skills considered adequate for jobs

Figure 10: **Reading skill levels by whether reading skills limit job opportunities**

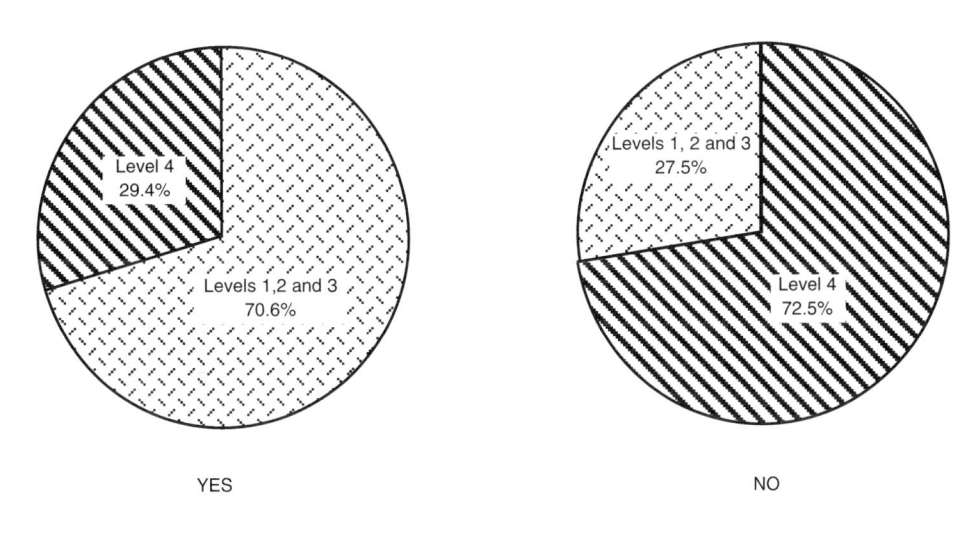

```
        YES                              NO

  Level 4                          Levels 1, 2 and 3
  29.4%                                 27.5%

  Levels 1,2 and 3                      Level 4
      70.6%                             72.5%
```

Skills limit job opportunities ?

Source: LSUDA.

Another valuable measure of workforce literacy in the survey, is: "Do you feel your reading skills in English/French are limiting your job opportunities?".

As Figure 10 demonstrates, 71 per cent of people who self-reported that their reading skills *were limiting* their job opportunities did, in fact, have inadequate reading skills. A similar percentage (73) of people who reported that their reading skills were *not* limiting their job opportunities had adequate reading skills[15].

LSUDA reading skill levels and other proxy indicators

Other indicators examined in the LSUDA survey that produce good results in predicting literacy levels are as follows: a history of a learning disability; the frequency with which one writes letters; a respondent's level of personal satisfaction with his/her reading skills; a respondent's perception as regards the adequacy of his/her literacy skills for everyday life; reading frequency of various types of materials (letters, blueprints, manuals, reports, lists, forms, and so forth) on the job; mother's educational attainment; and participation in voluntary and community organizations and in cultural life. These indicators are not discussed here. At this point, suffice it to say that the LSUDA survey contains a wide range of potentially strong surrogate measures of functional literacy, to be used alone or in combination with others. Our work in developing proxy indicators and measures has just begun. Nonetheless, we think that we have presented here strong evidence to demonstrate that this avenue of research has a great deal of potential.

The next step in our work will involve combining several of the strong proxy indicators into a predictor or factor model using association techniques such as log linear, logit, and principal components analysis. On the basis of the LSUDA data, we think that a simple proxy model could be constructed which might simulate as much as 90 per cent of the direct testing results. However, let us stress that such modelling can be done only because we have the direct measures available from the Statistics Canada survey. Direct measures provide a *benchmark* against which proxies can be refined. Proxies can never replace the benchmarks but they can work as interim surrogates as needed.

In addition, readers must be cautioned that the correlations we are finding, while strong, may be unique to Canada or may be generalizable only to other countries very similar to Canada. For instance, on the self-assessment and workforce literacy questions, the fact that public attention on the adult literacy issue is now high in Canada may be leading respondents to a more accurate self-rating. In the absence of many other direct assessment surveys, we cannot assess the strength of these proxies for other societies, although some of our hypotheses could be checked against the results of the upcoming U.S. surveys.

Additionally, we should note that some of the proposed proxy measures, such as learning disabilities, may be causal or antecedent, while others, such as parental levels of education, are correlates, and still others, such as library use, are consequences of weak literacy skills. It will be very important to explore the differences among causal, correlative, and consequent factors in the further construction of proxy models. A final word of caution is required, since our conclusions so far are only for reading skills, but adult literacy is really about the three skills of reading, writing, and numeracy. Much further developmental work is obviously needed.

Conclusion

Is there life left in the use of proxy measures when we know that direct assessments are so much better? This very much depends on the goals one wishes to achieve or advance. And most certainly, it depends on the selection of an appropriate technology of measurement to fulfill those goals.

A recent article by Daniel Wagner discusses in detail the issues which researchers must carefully examine in the development and selection of an appropriate measurement technology[16]. Our own research follows closely on Wagner's suggestion that a mixed technology of direct measures and indirect self-assessment measures can yield very strong results. In societies where the debate on adult functional illiteracy is well advanced, and where hard precise numbers are needed to inform and fuel that debate, there can be no doubt that direct skill assessment technology, while costly, will admirably succeed. In other societies, where interest in the issues is less developed (or not developed at all), or where the costs of direct assessment seem prohibitive, there are gains to be made both empirically, and from the point of view of advocacy, by carefully re-examining the utility of proxy measures. Such measures could be either derived from the secondary analysis of existing censuses or by commissioning new surveys and analyses using a selection of critical indicators which would constitute the principal components of a rigorous proxy model.

In summary, several options exist at different levels of cost, complexity, and comparability. Secondary analysis of any already available data sets, using proxy indicators similar to those discussed here, would be a start. Next in line would be to use a number of refined proxy indicators and to add them to other ongoing national surveys. Next would be a mix of proxies and direct assessment measures administered to a small sample in order to check the basic correlations, and then administered to a larger sample using a selection of the best proxy correlates. Even more advanced would be the full-scale direct assessment approach using a large sample, with accompanying proxy correlates, such as the Canadian and U.S. studies. And finally, at the highest level would be the integration of methodologies internationally, so that real comparative statistics on adult literacy can be developed world-wide, or at least for OECD Member states.

Many industrialized societies are in the grips of an adult literacy crisis, but the rate and speed of its public recognition in each society is highly variable. The institutional will to do something about the problem of adult illiteracy is also quite variable by country. Getting and keeping adult literacy on the public agenda of many industrialized societies will require that appropriate measurement technologies be available for different societal contexts and circumstances. The development of alternatives in the measurement of adult literacy, so that different technologies are both available and adaptable to specific societal contexts and circumstances, will aid us all. Some of those appropriate alternatives, we believe, may still reside in proxy measurements and models.

NOTES AND REFERENCES

1. This annex is based on a longer paper developed on the invitation of Paul Bélanger, Director of the UNESCO Institute for Education, as a contribution to a seminar held in Hamburg in November 1990 on the issue of functional adult literacy in both Eastern and Western European countries. The studies and data used in this annex almost exclusively reflect the empirical experiences in North American market economies. The question of the portability of these observations to other economies, even market ones, while certainly a critical consideration, is beyond the scope of this report. Only those who are intimate with the social, economic and institutional make-up of other industrial societies can evaluate if the suggestions made here are relevant to their specific contexts. The authors would particularly like to thank Thierry Noyelle, Ian Morrison, John Lowe, Stan Jones, Irwin Kirsch, Daniel Wagner, Jarl Bengtsson, Donald Hirsch, Scott Murray and others who attended the seminar for their useful comments on the draft paper. Readers who wish to have a copy of the original paper should write to the authors at The Department of the Secretary of State, Ottawa, Canada K1A OM5.

2. For a discussion of the concept of adult functional literacy and its pitfalls, see "Definitions, Estimates and Profiles of Literacy and Illiteracy", Working Paper No. 1, National Literacy Secretariat and Social Trends Analysis Directorate, Department of the Secretary of State, March 1, 1990.

3. Statistics Canada, *A National Literacy Skill Assessment Planning Report,* Special Surveys Group, April 1988.

4. L. Stedman and C. Kaestle, "Literacy and Reading Performance in the United States, from 1880 to the Present", *Reading Research Quarterly,* Winter 1987.

5. A.M. Thomas, "Adult Illiteracy in Canada – A Challenge", Occasional Paper No. 42, Canadian Commission for UNESCO, Ottawa, 1983.

6. *Ibid.,* p. 55.

7. M.E. Lalonde and G.A. Morey, "Functional Illiteracy and the Use of Statistics for Persons with less than Grade Nine Education", Statistics Canada, mimeo, 1987.

8. We are indebted to the Creative Research Group for this useful analytic distinction. See The Creative Research Group, *Literacy in Canada – A Research Report,* September 1987.

9. Lou Harris and Associates, *The 1971 National Reading Difficulty Index* (Washington, D.C.: National Reading Center, 1971); Adult Performance Level Project, *Final Report: The Adult Performance Level Study* (Washington, D.C.: U.S. Office of Education, 1977).

10. L. Stedman and C. Kaestle, "Literacy and Reading Performance", *op. cit.* (1987) p. 24.

11. U.S. Department of Education, *Report to Congress on Defining Literacy and the National Adult Literacy Survey,* July 1990.

12. Certain interesting reports have employed these measures because they were the only ones available for some time. See, for example, *Educationally Disadvantaged Adults: A Profile* (Toronto: Canadian Association for Adult Education, 1985).

13. The Gamma coefficient is as high as 0.83 using the following three categories of education: *a)* none; *b)* elementary; and *c)* high school or more. It was 0.67 using *i)* less than grade 5; *ii)* grades 5-8; *iii)* some high school; and *iv)* high school diploma or more.

14. EKOS Research Associates, *The Construction and Testing of a Reading Activity Index* (Ottawa: EKOS Research Associates, Inc., 1990).
15. Gamma coefficients were produced for these two workplace surrogate measures. They are 0.80 for the relationship between reading skills adequate for job and measured reading skill levels, and 0.73 for the relationship between the question on reading skills limiting job opportunities and measured reading skill levels. However, since in both of these correlations, one of the variables is binary (0,1), the results should be interpreted with some caution.
16. Daniel A. Wagner, "Literacy Assessment in the Third World: An Overview and Proposed Schema for Survey Use", *Comparative Education Review,* Vol. 34, No. 1, 1990.

WHERE TO OBTAIN OECD PUBLICATIONS – OÙ OBTENIR LES PUBLICATIONS DE L'OCDE

Argentina – Argentine
CARLOS HIRSCH S.R.L.
Galería Güemes, Florida 165, 4° Piso
1333 Buenos Aires   Tel. 30.7122, 331.1787 y 331.2391
Telegram: Hirsch-Baires
Telex: 21112 UAPE-AR. Ref. s/2901
Telefax:(1)331-1787

Australia – Australie
D.A. Book (Aust.) Pty. Ltd.
648 Whitehorse Road, P.O.B 163
Mitcham, Victoria 3132   Tel. (03)873.4411
Telefax: (03)873.5679

Austria – Autriche
OECD Publications and Information Centre
Schedestrasse 7
D-W 5300 Bonn 1 (Germany)   Tel. (49.228)21.60.45
Telefax: (49.228)26.11.04
Gerold & Co.
Graben 31
Wien 1   Tel. (0222)533.50.14

Belgium – Belgique
Jean De Lannoy
Avenue du Roi 202
B-1060 Bruxelles   Tel. (02)538.51.69/538.08.41
Telex: 63220   Telefax: (02) 538.08.41

Canada
Renouf Publishing Company Ltd.
1294 Algoma Road
Ottawa, ON K1B 3W8   Tel. (613)741.4333
Telex: 053-4783   Telefax: (613)741.5439
Stores:
61 Sparks Street
Ottawa, ON K1P 5R1   Tel. (613)238.8985
211 Yonge Street
Toronto, ON M5B 1M4   Tel. (416)363.3171
Federal Publications
165 University Avenue
Toronto, ON M5H 3B8   Tel. (416)581.1552
Telefax: (416)581.1743
Les Publications Fédérales
1185 rue de l'Université
Montréal, PQ H3B 3A7   Tel.(514)954-1633
Les Éditions La Liberté Inc.
3020 Chemin Sainte-Foy
Sainte-Foy, PQ G1X 3V6   Tel. (418)658.3763
Telefax: (418)658.3763

Denmark – Danemark
Munksgaard Export and Subscription Service
35, Nørre Søgade, P.O. Box 2148
DK-1016 København K   Tel. (45 33)12.85.70
Telex: 19431 MUNKS DK   Telefax: (45 33)12.93.87

Finland – Finlande
Akateeminen Kirjakauppa
Keskuskatu 1, P.O. Box 128
00100 Helsinki   Tel. (358 0)12141
Telex: 125080   Telefax: (358 0)121.4441

France
OECD/OCDE
Mail Orders/Commandes par correspondance:
2, rue André-Pascal
75775 Paris Cédex 16   Tel. (33-1)45.24.82.00
Bookshop/Librairie:
33, rue Octave-Feuillet
75016 Paris   Tel. (33-1)45.24.81.67
    (33-1)45.24.81.81
Telex: 620 160 OCDE
Telefax: (33-1)45.24.85.00 (33-1)45.24.81.76
Librairie de l'Université
12a, rue Nazareth
13100 Aix-en-Provence   Tel. 42.26.18.08
Telefax : 42.26.63.26

Germany – Allemagne
OECD Publications and Information Centre
Schedestrasse 7
D-W 5300 Bonn 1   Tel. (0228)21.60.45
Telefax: (0228)26.11.04

Greece – Grèce
Librairie Kauffmann
28 rue du Stade
105 64 Athens   Tel. 322.21.60
Telex: 218187 LIKA Gr

Hong Kong
Swindon Book Co. Ltd.
13 - 15 Lock Road
Kowloon, Hong Kong   Tel. 366.80.31
Telex: 50 441 SWIN HX   Telefax: 739.49.75

Iceland – Islande
Mál Mog Menning
Laugavegi 18, Pósthólf 392
121 Reykjavik   Tel. 15199/24240

India – Inde
Oxford Book and Stationery Co.
Scindia House
New Delhi 110001   Tel. 331.5896/5308
Telex: 31 61990 AM IN
Telefax: (11)332.5993
17 Park Street
Calcutta 700016   Tel. 240832

Indonesia – Indonésie
Pdii-Lipi
P.O. Box 269/JKSMG/88
Jakarta 12790   Tel. 583467
Telex: 62 875

Ireland – Irlande
TDC Publishers – Library Suppliers
12 North Frederick Street
Dublin 1   Tel. 744835/749677
Telex: 33530 TDCP EI   Telefax: 748416

Italy – Italie
Libreria Commissionaria Sansoni
Via Benedetto Fortini, 120/10
Casella Post. 552
50125 Firenze   Tel. (055)64.54.15
Telex: 570466   Telefax: (055)64.12.57
Via Bartolini 29
20155 Milano   Tel. 36.50.83
La diffusione delle pubblicazioni OCSE viene assicurata
dalle principali librerie ed anche da:
Editrice e Libreria Herder
Piazza Montecitorio 120
00186 Roma   Tel. 679.46.28
Telex: NATEL I 621427
Libreria Hoepli
Via Hoepli 5
20121 Milano   Tel. 86.54.46
Telex: 31.33.95   Telefax: (02)805.28.86
Libreria Scientifica
Dott. Lucio de Biasio 'Aeiou'
Via Meravigli 16
20123 Milano   Tel. 805.68.98
Telefax: 800175

Japan – Japon
OECD Publications and Information Centre
Landic Akasaka Building
2-3-4 Akasaka, Minato-ku
Tokyo 107   Tel. (81.3)3586.2016
Telefax: (81.3)3584.7929

Korea – Corée
Kyobo Book Centre Co. Ltd.
P.O. Box 1658, Kwang Hwa Moon
Seoul   Tel. (REP)730.78.91
Telefax: 735.0030

Malaysia/Singapore – Malaisie/Singapour
Co-operative Bookshop Ltd.
University of Malaya
P.O. Box 1127, Jalan Pantai Baru
59700 Kuala Lumpur
Malaysia   Tel. 756.5000/756.5425
Telefax: 757.3661
Information Publications Pte. Ltd.
Pei-Fu Industrial Building
24 New Industrial Road No. 02-06
Singapore 1953   Tel. 283.1786/283.1798
Telefax: 284.8875

Netherlands – Pays-Bas
SDU Uitgeverij
Christoffel Plantijnstraat 2
Postbus 20014
2500 EA's-Gravenhage   Tel. (070 3)78.99.11
Voor bestellingen: Tel. (070 3)78.98.80
Telex: 32486 stdru   Telefax: (070 3)47.63.51

New Zealand – Nouvelle-Zélande
GP Publications Ltd.
Customer Services
33 The Esplanade - P.O. Box 38-900
Petone, Wellington
Tel. (04)685-555   Telefax: (04)685-333

Norway – Norvège
Narvesen Info Center - NIC
Bertrand Narvesens vei 2
P.O. Box 6125 Etterstad
0602 Oslo 6   Tel. (02)57.33.00
Telex: 79668 NIC N   Telefax: (02)68.19.01

Pakistan
Mirza Book Agency
65 Shahrah Quaid-E-Azam
Lahore 3   Tel. 66839
Telex: 44886 UBL PK. Attn: MIRZA BK

Portugal
Livraria Portugal
Rua do Carmo 70-74, Apart. 2681
1117 Lisboa Codex   Tel.: 347.49.82/3/4/5
Telefax: (01) 347.02.64

Singapore/Malaysia – Singapour/Malaisie
See Malaysia/Singapore" – Voir «Malaisie/Singapour»

Spain – Espagne
Mundi-Prensa Libros S.A.
Castelló 37, Apartado 1223
Madrid 28001   Tel. (91) 431.33.99
Telex: 49370 MPLI   Telefax: 575.39.98
Libreria Internacional AEDOS
Consejo de Ciento 391
08009 - Barcelona   Tel. (93) 301-86-15
    Telefax: (93) 317-01-41
Llibreria de la Generalitat
Palau Moja, Rambla dels Estudis, 118
08002 - Barcelona
Tel. (93) 318.80.12 (Subscripcions)
(93) 302.67.23 (Publicacions)   Telefax: (93) 412.18.54

Sri Lanka
Centre for Policy Research
c/o Mercantile Credit Ltd.
55, Janadhipathi Mawatha
Colombo 1   Tel. 438471-9, 440346
Telex: 21138 VAVALEX CE   Telefax: 94.1.448900

Sweden – Suède
Fritzes Fackboksföretaget
Box 16356, Regeringsgatan 12
103 27 Stockholm   Tel. (08)23.89.00
Telex: 12387   Telefax: (08)20.50.21
Subscription Agency/Abonnements:
Wennergren-Williams AB
Nordenflychtsvägen 74, Box 30004
104 25 Stockholm   Tel. (08)13.67.00
Telex: 19937   Telefax: (08)618.62.32

Switzerland – Suisse
OECD Publications and Information Centre
Schedestrasse 7
D-W 5300 Bonn 1 (Germany)   Tel. (49.228)21.60.45
Telefax: (49.228)26.11.04
Librairie Payot
6 rue Grenus
1211 Genève 11   Tel. (022)731.89.50
Telex: 28356
Subscription Agency – Service des Abonnements
Naville S.A.
7, rue Lévrier
1201 Genève   Tél.: (022) 732.24.00
Telefax: (022) 738.48.03
Maditec S.A.
Chemin des Palettes 4
1020 Renens/Lausanne   Tel. (021)635.08.65
Telefax: (021)635.07.80
United Nations Bookshop/Librairie des Nations-Unies
Palais des Nations
1211 Genève 10   Tel. (022)734.14.73
Telex: 412962   Telefax: (022)740.09.31

Taiwan – Formose
Good Faith Worldwide Int'l. Co. Ltd.
9th Floor, No. 118, Sec. 2
Chung Hsiao E. Road
Taipei   Tel. 391.7396/391.7397
Telefax: (02) 394.9176

Thailand – Thaïlande
Suksit Siam Co. Ltd.
1715 Rama IV Road, Samyan
Bangkok 5   Tel. 251.1630

Turkey – Turquie
Kültur Yayinlari Is-Türk Ltd. Sti.
Atatürk Bulvari No. 191/Kat. 21
Kavaklidere/Ankara   Tel. 25.07.60
Dolmabahce Cad. No. 29
Besiktas/Istanbul   Tel. 160.71.88
Telex: 43482B

United Kingdom – Royaume-Uni
HMSO
Gen. enquiries   Tel. (071) 873 0011
Postal orders only:
P.O. Box 276, London SW8 5DT
Personal Callers HMSO Bookshop
49 High Holborn, London WC1V 6HB
Telex: 297138   Telefax: 071 873 2000
Branches at: Belfast, Birmingham, Bristol, Edinburgh,
Manchester

United States – États-Unis
OECD Publications and Information Centre
2001 L Street N.W., Suite 700
Washington, D.C. 20036-4910   Tel. (202)785.6323
Telefax: (202)785.0350

Venezuela
Libreria del Este
Avda F. Miranda 52, Aptdo. 60337, Edificio Galipán
Caracas 106   Tel. 951.1705/951.2307/951.1297
Telegram: Libreste Caracas

Yugoslavia – Yougoslavie
Jugoslovenska Knjiga
Knez Mihajlova 2, P.O. Box 36
Beograd   Tel.: (011)621.992
Telex: 12466 jk bgd   Telefax: (011)625.970

Orders and inquiries from countries where Distributors
have not yet been appointed should be sent to: OECD
Publications Service, 2 rue André-Pascal, 75775 Paris
Cedex 16, France.

Les commandes provenant de pays où l'OCDE n'a pas
encore désigné de distributeur devraient être adressées à :
OCDE, Service des Publications, 2, rue André-Pascal,
75775 Paris Cedex 16, France.

75880-7/91

OECD PUBLICATIONS, 2 rue André-Pascal, 75775 PARIS CEDEX 16
PRINTED IN FRANCE
(96 91 03 1) ISBN 92-64-13597-9 - No. 45751 1991